Humanistic Management
by Teamwork

Humanistic Management by Teamwork

An Organizational and Administrative Alternative for Academic Libraries

David A. Baldwin, Associate Professor
Director of Administrative Services
University of New Mexico General Library
Albuquerque, New Mexico

Robert L. Migneault, Professor
Dean of Library Services
University of New Mexico General Library
Albuquerque, New Mexico

1996
Libraries Unlimited, Inc.
Englewood, Colorado

LIBRARIES UNLIMITED, INC.
P.O. Box 6633
Englewood, CO 80155-6633
1-800-237-6124

Production Editor: Jason Cook
Copy Editor: Ramona Gault
Typesetting and Interior Design: Michael Florman
Indexer: Christine J. Smith

Library of Congress Cataloging-in-Publication Data

Baldwin, David A. (David Allen), 1946-
    Humanistic management by teamwork : an organizational and administrative alternative for academic libraries / David A. Baldwin and Robert LaLiberte Migneault.
        xvi, 187 p. 17 x 25 cm.
    Includes bibliographical references and index.
    ISBN 0-87287-981-X
    1. Academic libraries--Administration--Employee participation--United States. 2. Team librarianship--United States.
3. University of New Mexico. General Library--Administration.
4. Academic libraries--Administration--Employee participation--New Mexico--Albuquerque. 5. Team Librarianship--New Mexico--Albuquerque. I. Migneault, Robert LaLiberte. II. Title.
Z675.U5B28 1996
025.1'977--dc20   95-39937
                                                    CIP

To my mother, for her encouragement.
—David

To Joanne, my wife, who inspired me to write.
—Robert

•••••••• Contents

●●●●●●Acknowledgments

The authors are indebted to the faculty, staff, and student employees of the University of New Mexico General Library (UNMGL) and to the administration, faculty, staff, and students of the University of New Mexico for their support and understanding during the formative years of Humanistic Management by Teamwork (HMBT) at UNMGL. Many have provided insight, advice, and critiques of its implementation and operation. Without the cooperation and dedication of the library faculty and staff of UNMGL, Humanistic Management by Teamwork would still be only an idea instead of a reality in the library. Included in this book are many examples taken directly from policies drafted, discussed, and revised by the faculty and staff and now in effect. Thanks to all the many hardworking and dedicated participants in this "great experiment." Special thanks go to the department heads who persevered through the first few years of HMBT.

●●●●●●Introduction

This book provides an examination of teamwork as an organizational alternative to the traditional hierarchy in academic libraries. Today's libraries are facing challenges unparalleled in history. Automation has blurred the traditional public and technical services lines of the past. Access versus ownership, severe financial restraints in times of rapidly increasing costs, and rising service demands have required that academic libraries take a hard look at the status quo. The academic community demands that the library be a model of effective management before it can address cuts in serials, monographs, or services with credibility. Teamwork is an alternative that needs to be examined.

Teams have been in existence since hunting bands roamed in search of food during the last Ice Age. Only recently have organizations adopted teams as an organizational design. Teams are an integral component of Total Quality Management, a concept that is now being implemented throughout the country. Teamwork works, and Humanistic Management by Teamwork provides the added dimension of respect and dignity for everyone in the workplace.

People have great talents and abilities that often go untapped, and their intellectual potentialities are often poorly utilized in traditional library organizations. The library's most important assets, the faculty and staff, want and need to be treated with dignity and respect. Humanistic Management by Teamwork makes greater use of the talents of individuals organized in teams and is based on the principle of respect for each other in a complex organization, regardless of position. Humanistic Management by Teamwork provides a mechanism for reshaping the organization to meet the challenges of the twenty-first century.

The first chapter addresses the need to reshape the library organization and answers the question, "Why team management?" Chapter 2 looks closely at the pros and cons of team management. Chapters 3, 4, and 5 discuss the team-based organizational design and how it can be implemented. Chapters 6 through 10 describe how the University of New Mexico General Library (UNMGL) implemented and uses Humanistic Management by Teamwork in its operation. Included are discussions about staffing, communication, supervision, and performance appraisal as practiced at UNMGL. The last chapter presents a dialogue with Robert L. Migneault, UNMGL Dean of Library

Services and architect of Humanistic Management by Teamwork. Bibliographies are presented at the end of each chapter.

Certain features of Humanistic Management by Teamwork make the library that is using it different from libraries with hierarchical systems. These differences involve the management team structure; the outcome-based performance appraisal system, which includes upward evaluations; the team management library's committee structure; the library faculty organization; and the empowerment of employees. It is the authors' experience that the organizational and administrative structure of HMBT positively affects the climate of the library, fostering trust, support, and respect, which in turn make the library a more humane workplace.

•••••••• Chapter 1

Why Management by Teamwork?

"Can anybody remember when
the times were not hard and money not scarce?"
—Ralph Waldo Emerson (1803–1882)

Challenges Facing Organizations

Modern society is a complex of organizations that include family, school, government, church, business, and industry. An organization is simply the arrangement and utilization of human, financial, and material resources for the accomplishment of goals. The waking hours of almost every person are spent within the structures and processes of organizations.

Sometime during their lifetimes, all organizations are faced with difficult, seemingly unsolvable problems. Those problems that must be addressed by the members of organizations may be problems of organizational output, consequences, processes, or dynamics.

When a service-oriented organization fails to meet its users' demands, change is needed. When the organizational means by which output is achieved drop below an acceptable level, members begin to plan for change. The demands placed on libraries outstrip their ability to adequately meet those demands. In addition, the information explosion, coupled with the inability of parent institutions to sustain needed levels of funding, requires that academic and research libraries critically examine their organizational structures. Today's academic and research libraries are organizations faced with the most challenging problems and opportunities in their long history.

1

Challenges Facing Academic Libraries

The Research Library Committee, jointly sponsored by the Association of American Universities, the Council on Library Resources, the American Council of Learned Societies, and the Social Science Research Council, issued its *Statement* regarding academic libraries in May 1990. The following is from the Research Library Committee *Statement*:

> The form of future library service will be shaped by how well librarians and other library information specialists cope with the sheer quantity of published material, the growing number of print and non-print formats used to store information, escalating requirements of users for access to everything of importance, new and rising costs, and the structural changes in the system of scholarly communication brought on by the interrelated technologies that are transforming how information is stored, organized, processed, and transmitted. Fortunately, librarians [and other library information specialists] have a strong record of accomplishment. They have cooperatively developed computerized bibliographic systems that identify and locate millions of publications. They have pioneered in the application to library operations and services. Most important, they have demonstrated that they can join forces to attack, on a national level, such intractable problems as preservation.[1]

Regarding the library in the university structure, the Research Library Committee reminds us that:

> The scope of library responsibilities reaches across all academic levels and affects all fields of study. Research libraries, by their nature, not only respond to individual users; they also influence what users do. The work of universities is inseparable from the substance of libraries, and the continuity inherent in the scholarly enterprise is reflected in every aspect of library operations. Libraries can be active contributors to the work of universities, but only if librarians are constructively involved in the development of academic programs. It is essential that the library be linked effectively to the [teaching and research faculty], to the university planning structure, and to academic and administrative governance, and that each of those university sectors does what is required to make the process of setting policies and priorities work.

(Research Library Committee, *Statement*, May 1990)

This day and age offers many challenges and opportunities for the modern-day academic research-oriented librarian. Consider the opinions shared by the members of the Research Library Committee:

> The university community obviously expects that library management will be responsible, imaginative, and productive. Collections must be built and maintained, needs of users met, and operating capabilities constantly refined to contain costs and assure that future as well as present interests are served. University library obligations to the past, present, and future have converged with great force. Large portions of accumulated collections are physically fragile; current publication volume is expanding worldwide, and the expectations of users are honed by what they now see as technically possible. More fundamentally, it is not clear that the research library of today can be a paradigm for the twenty-first century library. The rise of new fields of inquiry and the shifting organization of knowledge into new configurations present a demanding challenge for libraries, which conduct their collecting and bibliographic work on an historically established base. Further, uncertainty about organization and operations is implicit in a future where the extent and influence of innovation in telecommunications and electronic publishing are essentially unknown. The years ahead will be demanding ones, but the foundation on which to build is largely in place. The members of the Research Library Committee . . . recognize the difficulties libraries face, but also see an exceptional opportunity to make constructive change and assure for academic research libraries, individually and collectively, their unique, educationally important role into the twenty-first century.
>
> (Research Library Committee, *Statement*, May 1990)

The academic library must be a model of organizational effectiveness in the university. The research library must resolve problems relating to information provision, developing and implementing new ways to provide access to services and collections in the light of diminishing resources, while at the same time offering its faculty and staff a humane, caring work environment. Team management is being implemented throughout the corporate world not only to provide a better work environment for employees but also to improve productivity, capitalizing on the need of workers for more participation in decision making. For many libraries, this means changing the organizational structure.

Change Strategies

When organizations are faced with problems that call for change and wish to demonstrate that action is being taken, they may adopt one of the following change strategies:

1. Increased control. In times of stress and crisis, a common approach is to push employees harder, expecting greater productivity and cracking down on poor performance.

2. Cutbacks. In order to demonstrate greater responsibility and improved profits, organizations cut back on various resources, including personnel, budgets, or inventories. Management may often eliminate services or departments, although expecting that productivity will remain unchanged.

3. Incentives. If inadequate performance is suspected, incentives are offered on the assumption that personal benefit and financial rewards are motivators for employees.

4. Motivators. Managers may try to solve problems by devising activities such as contests, competitions between departments, propaganda campaigns, special awards, and recognition programs.

5. Consultants. The hope is that an outside expert can quickly identify the ills and offer solutions to the problems.

Use of these various strategies has mixed results in solving organizational problems. When an organization composed of human beings arranged together to reach goals finds that it is no longer capable of solving its problems or reaching its goals, it may need to search for a way to reshape itself. One alternative is management by teamwork.

Teamwork

Team management is an alternative for revitalizing the organization. Systems have a tendency to become established, routinized, and institutionalized around certain procedures, methods, and processes that may no longer meet today's demands. If the system serves to keep people at a low level or is restrictive and authoritarian, or both, the organization can be reshaped to release human potential through management by teamwork. Some of the positive outcomes of team management are the following:

1. Climate of high social support. Team members experience a supportive environment that builds and maintains their sense of personal worth and importance. It can be a climate where there are a high level of trust, feelings of concern, and high self-esteem among members.

2. Open communication. The organization makes all relevant information available to decision makers and members.

3. Creative problem solving. Through participative and shared management, members are encouraged to engage in finding creative solutions to organizational problems.

4. Commitment. There is high commitment on the part of members to the organization's goals and to supporting and implementing decisions.

5. Achievement of individual and organizational goals. Members are encouraged to set and achieve individual and team goals that are consistent with and supportive of organizational goals.

6. Interdependence. Team members make the greatest use of their own individual resources as they use the resources of the team. The opposite of interdependence is dependency, such as in a hierarchy, where employees depend on authorities and respond to demands of authority.

7. Team effort. The result of high interdependence, team effort nevertheless does not mean management by committee. Members have their own roles on the team and feel responsible for their own work as well as the work of the team.

Why should library directors consider team management as an organization design? On a practical level, team management at its best is highly effective and efficient, making excellence an obtainable objective. Ethically, team management dispels apathy—the curse often found in the workplace. Humanistically, team management offers participants the opportunity to celebrate and fulfill the grand potential of humankind.

Comparing Hierarchical and Team Management Environments

The traditional hierarchical organization and the team management environment in libraries differ from one another in many ways. To see the differences, compare the following scenarios at ABC Library, a traditional hierarchy, and CBA Library, a library reshaped by team management. Names and places have been

changed to protect the innocent, but all scenarios are based on actual situations.

ABC University enrolls 20,000 students, with half of those in
graduate programs. Its library is a member of the Association of Research Libraries, with a collection of 2.1 million volumes. The staff at
ABC University Library total 212 full-time employees (FTE), with 57
of those being tenure-track library faculty. The library is organized
in the traditional manner, with four divisions: public services, which
includes seven branch libraries; technical services; collection development; and administrative services. Each of the divisions is headed
by an associate dean, who oversees from two to 11 departments,
each with a department head. The staff in the divisions are classified
into clerical, technical, and paraprofessional grades established by
the university and the state employment system.

CBA University enrolls 24,000 students, with half of those in
graduate programs. The CBA library is a member of the Association
of Research Libraries, with a collection of 1.9 million volumes. The
staff at CBA University Library total 191 FTE, with 46 tenure-track
library faculty. The library is organized as a team management library. The department heads report directly to the dean of library
services, and the staff in the departments are classified into clerical,
technical, and professional grades established by the library and the
university.

SCENARIO 1: ABC Library—Lines of Communication

Donna is a technical assistant II in the Art and Art History Library, a branch of ABC Library. Her job is to handle adds, withdrawals, and transfers as well as to work several shifts at the
reference desk and assist with circulation as needed. Joanne is a
cataloging tech III in the central cataloging department at the Main
Library. She does transfers for the major collection at Main. Donna
has been trying to resolve a knotty problem relating to the transfer
of an architectural art series to the Architecture Library across campus. Donna describes the problem to her supervisor, who is unfamiliar with the transfer process because he has just been reassigned
to Art and Art History from Special Collections, where he supervised the manuscripts collections. Donna's supervisor discusses the
problem with the associate director of the Art and Art History Library. The associate director consults with the director, Mrs. Harper,
who promises to see the associate director for public services. After Mrs. Harper's phone call, the associate director for public services takes the problem to the associate director for technical
services. This associate director consults with the head of cataloging, who calls in the head of bibliographic control. The supervisor of bibliographic maintenance receives a visit from the head of

bibliographic control two days after she returns from her fantastic two-week vacation in Mexico. The supervisor of bibliographic maintenance, who never thought that the Art and Art History Library should be a branch, waits for Joanne to return from her class and describes the problem. Joanne, who has been doing transfers for over four years, knows exactly what is to be done and tells her supervisor. The supervisor returns to the head of bibliographic control with the solution to Donna's problem. The head of bibliographic control relays the answer to the director of cataloging, who leaves a message for the associate director for technical services, who is due to return from a conference in three days. The associate directors meet for coffee. The associate director for public services, armed with the transfer solution, visits the Art and Art History Library (later the staff will recount to one another where they were when they sighted the associate director for public services in their library). In a prearranged meeting with Mrs. Harper, the associate director for public services relays the solution. The director of the Art and Art History Library goes next door to the associate director, who duly notes the solution. The associate director goes to the processing office to find the supervisor of technical operations, who has taken three days of medical leave to care for his mother. Meanwhile, the associate director for administrative services has, with the assistance of the library personnel office and the university human relations office, processed Donna's reassignment papers. Donna has been promoted to technical assistant III at the Science and Engineering Library. The architectural art series sits on the book truck near the technical assistant II desk, awaiting transfer, while the paperwork is prepared to get approval to post the vacant position. When the new person is hired, the process will begin anew. A bit far-fetched perhaps, but does it sound familiar?

SCENARIO 2: CBA Library—Lines of Communication

John is a library technical assistant II in the Fine Arts Library, a branch of the CBA Library. His job is to handle adds, withdrawals, and transfers as well as to work several shifts at the reference desk and assist with circulation as needed. Yolanda is a library specialist III and team leader for the bibliographic maintenance team in the catalog department. John has been trying to resolve a knotty problem relating to the transfer of an architectural art series to the Architecture Library across campus. John phones Yolanda, who gives him a tentative answer to his question and asks him to bring the material to the online catalog committee meeting the next day so they can discuss it after the meeting. John and Yolanda both know that when they have questions or concerns, they can contact anyone in the organization, from the clerk in the mail room to the dean, all of whom are colleagues in the team management environment. This scenario is repeated many times daily in different ways in the team management library.

SCENARIO 3: ABC Library—Chain of Command

It is the end of the semester at ABC University, and the circulation department at the library is getting all of the books back. The problem, as noted by Lee, the stacks supervisor, is that there are not enough book trucks in the department for all the student employees to use in reshelving. Lee has noticed that members of the cataloging staff have managed to surround their desks with half-filled book trucks that never seem to move. Lee describes the book truck shortage to his supervisor, the head of the circulation department. Perhaps the library could replace some of the catalogers' book trucks with shelving because, after all, what they have done is use trucks as permanent shelving. The circulation department head agrees with Lee and goes to see her boss, the director of access services. The access services director thinks it is a great idea. The stacks maintenance students could put up shelving for the catalogers and free needed book trucks. The director of access services visits the office of the associate director for public services. The associate director quickly vetoes the idea, declaring that the catalogers would never give up their trucks. In truth, the problem is that the two associate directors are feuding over the director's most recent personnel allocation decision, made in favor of technical services. The director of access services informs the head of circulation that the catalogers will not give up their book trucks. The head of circulation tells Lee to forget about getting extra book trucks and just make do with the book trucks available.

SCENARIO 4: CBA Library—Chain of Command

It is the end of the semester at CBA University, and the circulation department is getting all of the books back. The problem, as noted by Judy, the stacks supervisor, is that there are not enough book trucks in the department for student employees to use in reshelving. Judy checks with the circulation department head and then goes to the dean's office. Judy writes a note and hands it to the administrative assistant, who is editor of the weekly newsletter. It reads as follows:

Book Trucks Needed

The circulation department is experiencing its end of the semester onslaught of returned books. We need your help. If you can spare one or more book trucks (with working wheels), please contact Judy at the main library circulation desk. We promise to return them within two weeks. Thanks.

The day after distribution of the newsletter, Judy has commitments for the loan of 13 book trucks from five departments and branches, including four book trucks from the catalog department, all with wheels. There are no bureaucratic walls that divide departments in the team management environment.

SCENARIO 5: ABC Library—Personnel Decisions

At ABC Library, Janet returns to her office in the Business Library to find exactly what she has dreaded most. There, lying on her chair, is a resignation letter from Carl. He is not her most efficient and effective employee, but without him, there is no one to handle reserves in the circulation department. Now Janet must find a new reserves supervisor. She phones the associate director for public services, but he is away from the office, so she begins to compose her request in her head. She knows that the process will involve not only a well-written justification but also several strategy meetings with Don, the associate director for public services. Don will take her request and their strategy to the administrative council, composed of the director and the associate directors for public services, technical services, collections, and administration. She has doubts about Don. It seems that nothing public services needs is ever approved. Maybe he is not strong enough. Technical Services seems to get everything it wants, and the collections department always seems more important than the service's department when it comes to reallocation of resources. When Don fails to get something for a department, the department head has to answer to the staff. The last time, the administrative council took three student positions from circulation and gave them to acquisitions. All Janet can do is try. After several weeks, the request is ready for presentation to the council. That morning, Janet is anxious about the outcome. Carl is gone and Janet is spending more time in the reserves area, trying to keep things under control. The phone call comes later that afternoon. Don is sorry it did not go better, but Carl's position has been frozen. The student budget is overspent and the money is needed for student employees, according to Don. Janet will have to try to get by. Janet longs for the time when public services had a stronger advocate.

SCENARIO 6: CBA Library—Personnel Decisions

David knew it was only a matter of time until Dorothy won her promotion. She had interviewed for the library specialist position at the Main Library and he had given her a good recommendation. Now he has her resignation on his desk. As head of circulation, David reviews the process of replacement in his mind. He will send a written request to the personnel review committee with a description of the position and a justification for refilling. The committee comprises four exempt (union) and one nonexempt (non-union) staff members and four library faculty members, three of whom are department heads. They will review the request and make a written recommendation to the library management team. If there are concerns expressed in the committee or suggestions on how to approach the vacancy differently, he will be asked to meet with them to discuss his request. The recommendation to the library management team will be attached to the meeting agenda and will include a fiscal implications statement. When personnel items are considered in the closed portion of the meeting, he will be able to provide additional information as needed. He also knows that the committee's recommendations, although discussed by the library management team, are usually approved. Because he and other members of the team receive regular budget updates, he knows that there will be no surprises about budgetary shortfalls that will affect his vacancy. Shortly after the weekly personnel review committee meeting, David gets a call from the chair. She tells him that the committee has reviewed his request. It believes that the position was classified incorrectly and it wishes to recommend that the position be posted one grade higher. The chair asks David if he agrees with the committee's assessment. He does. There are funds available in the budget to cover the higher-level position. At the next library management team meeting, the recommendation of the committee is approved.

SCENARIO 7: ABC Library—Professional Travel

Jim is the audio technician in the branch Music Library. His duties include the supervision of the listening room and maintenance of the audio equipment and the sound recording collection. He reports to Maryanne, the associate director of the Music Library. Jim receives an announcement of the annual music library association conference. Although he is not a librarian, he is a member of the organization. After some calculation, he figures he could attend the conference in a nearby state for about $500. He knows that he will have to request annual leave to attend. His boss will probably also attend with at least partial funding and will just report the absence from work as professional leave. Of course Maryanne will have to request travel funds and leave through the director of the Music Library. The director will give the request to the library system-wide associate director for public services, who will have to get approval at an administrative council meeting. She will not know what discussion will take place but will be told the outcome. Jim considers his personal finances and wonders how he will be able to scrape up $500.

SCENARIO 8: CBA Library—Professional Travel

Greg is the audio technician in the branch Music Library. His duties include the supervision of the listening room and maintenance of the audio equipment and the sound recording collection. He reports to Carlos, the associate director of the Music Library. Greg receives an announcement of the annual music library association conference. Although he is not a librarian, he is a member of the organization. After some calculation, he figures he could attend the conference in a nearby state for about $500. He takes out his copy of the library professional staff advisory council professional enrichment awards guidelines. In order to apply for travel support, he knows that the conference has to be job related. The conference always has a heavy emphasis on sound recordings. Greg completes the application for professional enrichment funds and submits it to the council. He knows that if it is approved, he will receive up to 90 percent funding and will attend on university time. He can still take that long-awaited trip to the Grand Canyon with his annual leave. Carlos also receives the announcement. He knows that he can request professional enrichment funds from the faculty's professional enrichment committee, appointed by the faculty committee on committees. He understands that his level of funding support will be less than Greg's, but he is aware that he must attend the conference as part of his faculty service requirements. Carlos also looks forward to meeting with his friends and colleagues from across the country. Both Greg and Carlos know that their requests will be given full consideration by committees of their peers. Maybe they can share a room.

SCENARIO 9: ABC Library—Equipment Purchases

Rebecca is a library specialist II in the map room in the branch Science and Engineering Library. For the past three months she has been trying to find a way to file aeronautical charts and topographic maps in the cramped files. Rebecca explains to Sarah, the map room head, that they have to get one more legal-size file cabinet and one more map cabinet. Sarah explains that in order to get the cabinets, she will have to request that the director of the Science and Engineering Library talk to the library system-wide associate director for public services. Her request is put in writing and discussed with the associate director. He reminds Sarah that all equipment requests have to be reviewed and approved by the administrative council and that the associate director for public services has a folder full of public services equipment requests. He assures her that he will include the two cabinets but that equipment requests will not be considered until spring. Sarah returns to the map room, trying to figure out a way to break the news to Rebecca that she had better find a way to file the charts and maps, because there will be no file cabinets for months, if ever.

SCENARIO 10: CBA Library—Equipment Purchases

Ken is a library specialist II in the map room in the branch Science and Engineering Library. He has tried everything he can think of to find a way to file aeronautical charts and topographic maps in the cramped files. Ken explains to Michelle, the map room head, that they have to get one more legal-size file cabinet and one more map cabinet. Michelle asks Ken to put his requests in writing, one for the file cabinet and one for the map cabinet. Michelle knows that the director of the Science and Engineering Library can approve the purchase of a legal-size file cabinet, but that the request for a map cabinet will exceed his signing authority limits. The director signs Ken's $300 file cabinet request and sends it to the main library fiscal office for processing. The branch library director requests that the map cabinet purchase be put on the agenda of the next system-wide library management team meeting, when he can explain why it is needed. Team members will consider this request in light of overall library needs. Because all members of the team receive regular budget updates, they can determine whether or not the library has the funds available for the map cabinet and decide its priority for purchase. If Michelle and Ken's request for a map cabinet is not approved, at least they will know the reasons.

Management by Teamwork Is Not for Everyone

Management by teamwork is not a panacea. Poor managers will probably be poor managers in the team management environment. Hiring, training, and development of effective managers are critical. Uncommitted, uncaring employees may be uncommitted and uncaring in the team management environment, but management by teamwork provides the opportunity to change some of those employees. An organization full of mistrust and suspicion will not be automatically cured by team management, especially if it is a nominal arrangement. In all likelihood, management by teamwork in such an environment will fail miserably.

Teamwork does not come without hard work. If the solution to the organizational problems is teamwork, those problems will not disappear without wholesale commitment to the team approach. In fact, new problems will arise that call for new and creative solutions. Management by teamwork in academic libraries provides an organizational design that serves as a foundation for addressing the critical problems described earlier in this chapter.

Bibliography

Chu, Yen-an. *Organizational Teamwork in High-Speed Management.* Albany, N.Y.: State University of New York Press, 1985.

Dalziel, Murray M., and Stephen C. Schoonover. *Changing Ways: A Practical Tool for Implementing Change Within Organizations.* New York: AMACOM, 1988.

De Gennaro, Richard. *Libraries, Technology, and the Information Marketplace.* Boston: G. K. Hall, 1987.

Drucker, Peter F. "The Coming of the New Organization." *Harvard Business Review* 66, no. 1 (January/February 1988): 45–53.

Dyer, William G. *Insight to Impact: Strategies for Interpersonal and Organizational Change.* Provo, Utah: Brigham Young University Press, 1976.

Evans, G. Edward. "Research Libraries in 2010." In *Research Libraries: The Past 25 Years, the Next 25 Years,* edited by Taylor E. Hubbard, 77–94. Boulder, Colo.: Colorado Associated University Press, 1986.

Garson, Barbara. *The Electronic Sweatshop: How Computers Are Transforming the Office of the Future into the Factory of the Past.* New York: Simon & Schuster, 1988.

Goodman, Paul S. *Designing Effective Work Groups.* San Francisco: Jossey-Bass, 1991.

Harris, Philip R. *Management in Transition: Transforming Managerial Practices and Organizational Strategies for a New Work Culture.* San Francisco: Jossey-Bass, 1985.

Johnston, William B., and Arnold E. Packer. *Workforce 2000: Work and Workers for the 21st Century.* Indianapolis, Ind.: Hudson Institute, 1987.

Leontief, Wassily, and Faye Duchin. *The Future Impact of Automation on Workers.* London: Oxford University Press, 1986.

Lynch, Beverly P., ed. *The Academic Library in Transition: Planning for the 1990's.* New York: Neal-Schuman, 1989.

Mangnani, Nanette Brey. *Building Organizational Effectiveness Through Participation and Teamwork.* New York: PACT, 1992.

Mason, Marilyn Gell. "Trends Challenging the Library: Technological, Economic, Social, Political." In *The ALA Yearbook of Library and Information Services*. Vol. 11, 1–6. Chicago: American Library Association, 1986.

Ministry of Foreign Affairs. *Japan & the United States: Teamwork Today and Tomorrow*. Tokyo: Ministry of Foreign Affairs, 1993.

Nicholas, Ted. *Secrets of Entrepreneurial Leadership: Building Top Performance Through Trust & Teamwork*. Chicago: Enterprise Dearborn, 1993.

Research Library Committee. *Statement*. Report jointly sponsored by the Association of American Universities, the Council on Library Resources, the American Council of Learned Societies, and the Social Science Research Council. May 1990.

Riggs, Donald E., and Gordon A. Sabine. *Libraries in the '90's: What the Leaders Expect*. Phoenix, Ariz.: Oryx Press, 1988.

Sashkin, Marshall. *The New Teamwork: Developing and Using Cross-Function Teams*. New York: American Management Association, 1994.

Shaiken, Harley. *Work Transformed: Automation and Labor in the Computer Age*. New York: Holt, Rinehart & Winston, 1985.

Shonk, James H. *Team-Based Organizations: Developing a Successful Team Environment*. Homewood, Ill.: Business One-Irwin, 1992.

Notes

1. Research Library Committee, *Statement*, report jointly sponsored by the Association of American Universities, the Council on Library Resources, the American Council of Learned Societies, and the Social Science Research Council, May 1990.

●●●●●●●●Chapter 2

Pros and Cons of Teamwork

"Time is a great teacher, but
unfortunately it kills all its pupils."
—Hector Berlioz (1803–1869)

Looking at Team Management

Teams in libraries are becoming the "in" thing to have. As libraries face downsizing or "right sizing," demands for more participation by all levels of staff, and the realization that participation is desirable, administrators are taking a closer look at team management. Total Quality Management, for example, imposed from higher levels of administration, uses quality teams and the teamwork approach. For many hierarchical libraries, a more horizontal organization seems an appropriate, almost inevitable goal.

This book describes the positive aspects of teams and teamwork and how teams can be effectively implemented and used in libraries, citing specifically the experiment that has been fully operational at the University of New Mexico General Library (UNMGL) since 1986. In this chapter we will detail the pros and cons of team management for libraries.

Teams in Academe Are "Not Attainable"

In his book *Academic Librarianship in a Transformational Age*, library consultant Allen Veaner contends that an academic community cannot be made into a team:

Fundamentally, team structures spell the redistribution of power in an organization. In the strongly elitist and highly stratified microcosm of academe, however, all members of the group are not peers. It is quite impossible to give everyone an equal voice in programmatic affairs. As stated

15

[in another chapter], an academic community cannot and should not be turned into a team; the concept implies a degree of unity and intimate cooperation that is not attainable in academe. The stratified groupings in an academic library have their own informal structures, separate agendas, group and individual goals, all of which are more in conflict than in congruence. To claim that such diversity can be welded into a team is more than wishful thinking, it is nonsense. Within this arena of conflict, management is an integrating force, acting to assure the achievement of institutional mission, goals, and objectives in spite of all of these differences. Managers are expected to find or invent ways to get different groups of employees to work together as a coordinated group. Among other things, management is paid to do exactly that. . . .[1]

Traditional middle managers typically find team structures threatening and adapt uneasily. Unions continue to view labor-management relations as basically adversarial and see team setups as a possible deterrent to unionization; thus they are slow to give up their rights. The new paradigm's highest rates of success occur in new plants or offices where semicollegial team structures can be installed without the agonies of trying to resocialize an established middle management and/or persuade unions to surrender some power.[2]

Can team management be implemented successfully in academe? If by successful, one means having a favorable outcome or having obtained something desired or intended, seeing is believing. The experience at UNMGL demonstrates that team management can be implemented successfully in academe. The implementation of team management in the library may not have had a significant impact on the rest of the university. However, its impact on academe, if you will, is that the library is known as a well-managed college facility with high morale and a highly respected faculty and staff. It is not the library's purpose to change management structures throughout academe as a whole, only to be effective in its own mission.

Disadvantages of Using Teams

Based on research in the field and the experience at UNMGL, the authors have discovered potential shortcomings of the team management approach. Teams in academe can experience burnout and become complacent, exhausting their ideas without fresh input from new members. The more cohesive a group becomes, the more likely it is that members will not censor what they say out of fear of antagonizing the leader or other members. Members also may deliberately censor themselves because of the desire to maintain group unity and to adhere to its norms.

When the team has a high degree of cohesiveness and esprit de corps, its members may fall victim to groupthink. The process is characterized by a marked decrease in the exchange of potentially conflicting data and an unwillingness to critically examine those data. In their desire for unanimity, team members may become insulated in their thinking, discounting negative information from outsiders, or they may reach consensus simply to please the boss. Groupthink may be diagnosed when the following symptoms are present:

1. The team has the illusion of unanimity and an emphasis on team play.

2. The team views the "opposition" as generally inept, incompetent, and incapable of countering any action by the group.

3. Group members censor themselves, overt disagreements are avoided, faulty assumptions go unchallenged, and personal doubts are suppressed in the interest of group harmony.

4. Collective rationalization is used when an agreed-upon decision is clearly unworkable.

5. The team has self-appointed mind guards within the group who prevent unwelcome ideas and adverse information that may threaten unanimity.

6. The team applies direct pressure on dissenting members who threaten consensus.

7. The team develops a sense of self-righteousness that leads members to believe their actions are moral and ethical, thus allowing them to ignore ethical or moral objections to their behavior.

8. The team exhibits a shared feeling of unassailability, marked by a high degree of esprit de corps, implicit faith in the wisdom of the group, and optimism that leads the team to believe it can take excessive risks.

There are other criticisms of teams, as well. A team does not possess clarity unless the team leader creates it. A team has poor stability. Its economy is low; a team demands continuing attention to its management, to the relationships of people within the task force, to assigning people to their jobs, to explanation, deliberation, communication, and so on. A large part of the energy of all the members goes into keeping things running. Although everybody on the team understands the common task, team members do not always understand their own specific tasks. They may be so interested in what others are doing that they pay inadequate attention to their own assignments.[3]

Teams do only a little better than straight functional organizations in preparing people for higher management responsibilities or in testing their performance. A team makes for neither clear communications nor clear decision making. The whole group must work constantly on explaining both to itself and to managers throughout the rest of the organization what it is trying to do, what it is working on, and what it has accomplished. The team must constantly make sure that the decisions that need to be made are brought into the open, when it is much easier to do the opposite. Teams fail, and the failure rate has been high, primarily because they do not impose on themselves the self-discipline and responsibility that are required as a result of the high degree of freedom team organization gives. No task force can be permissive and function. This is the reason why the same young, educated people who clamor for teamwork so often in reality tend to resist it. It makes tremendous demands on self-discipline.[4]

But the greatest limitation for the team structure is size. Teams work best when there are few members. The aboriginal hunting band had seven to 15 members. So do the teams in team sports. Although athletic team rosters may be large, participation of more than a dozen members simultaneously is rare. If a team gets much larger than the aboriginal hunting band, it becomes unwieldy. "The team's strengths, such as flexibility and the sense of responsibility of the members, attenuate. Its limitations—lack of clarity, communication problems, overconcern with the internal mechanism and internal relationship—become crippling weaknesses."[5]

To summarize the argument against management by teamwork in libraries:

1. Administrators and middle managers do not wish to share authority, do not have a unity of purpose, and will not cooperate in the elitist, stratified academic environment. They do not possess teamwork skills or knowledge.

2. Unions dislike teams because they disrupt the adversarial relationship between labor and management.

3. Teams are inefficient because they demand continuing attention to their development, operation, and maintenance. They do not, on their own, make for clear communication or decision making. Teams tend toward inaction until consensus is reached. Teams must continually explain themselves and may succumb to groupthink. The size of teams is a severe limitation, and all teams are prone to burnout.

4. Team members may ignore their own work when paying attention to team activity. They may not have the self-discipline or
skills required of teamwork. Empowered employees may not
know their limits, and outsiders view teamwork with distrust
and dismay. Who is in charge?

All of these arguments against teamwork are grounded in low
expectations and a low regard for the individual. The authors
contend that the benefits far outweigh the negatives of team
management.

Advantages of Using Teams

People have great talents that are often barely tapped by organizations. Work groups, task teams, matrix organizations, project
teams, and the team management environment offer opportunities
for people to accomplish more by making better use of their talents
and by reducing barriers to communication and cooperation. Innovative patterns of organization call for a high degree of enlightened
and supportive leadership from top management.

Success is not guaranteed just because individuals are organized
in teams, but there are clear advantages to individuals and the organization in the team management approach. Both scientific research and successful experience by managers indicate that
individuals functioning as members of a team can perform better
than those working alone.[6] Individuals working as a team can usually pool their ideas and come up with solutions to problems more
effectively than can a single person working on the same problems.
Not only can a team generate better ideas, but also the chances that
decisions will be successfully implemented are much improved.
Teamwork recognizes that individuals assembled into teams can
maximize their potential. A major advantage of teamwork is the
positive feeling generated in team members. Individuals have high
self-esteem in cohesive teams. Cohesiveness in groups also increases
the power of the team over the individual, which has both positive
and negative aspects. Team membership has many benefits for individuals, but teams must be aware of groupthink and take care to
avoid it.

Adaptability of Teams

The team organization has great adaptability. In a team, everyone
knows the work of the whole and holds himself or herself responsible
for it. The team is highly receptive to experimentation, new ideas,
and new ways of doing things.

Its size limitation determines the scope of applicability of the team principle in management. It is the best available design principle for top management work—probably the only appropriate design principle for top management work. It is the preferred design principle for innovative work. But for most operating work, the team is not appropriate by itself as the design principle of organization. It is a complement—though a badly needed one. It may well be that team organization will function more effectively and enable the organization to do what its designers had hoped for. But the area where team design as a complement to functional organization is likely to make the greatest contribution is in knowledge work. Knowledge work by definition is specialized work. A good deal of knowledge work will undoubtedly be organized on a strictly functional basis. A good deal will also be done by individuals who, in effect, are an organizational component by themselves.[7]

Teams are the best means for overcoming functional insulation and parochialism. Any career professional should serve on a few teams during his or her working life.[8]

Teams Empower Individuals in Flattened Hierarchies

Peter Block, in his book *The Empowered Manager*, suggests radically changing the hierarchy in order to develop an entrepreneurial organization. Among the suggestions Block makes are to flatten out the organization, reverse the performance appraisal process, and introduce self-managing teams.[9]

Flattening the organization reduces the layers of staffing from top to bottom, making individuals more responsible for the success of the organization. In the team management environment, layers of administration and barriers between divisions are removed. Reversing the performance appraisal process serves to allow the supervisor and those being supervised to have a common interest in each other's success. Evaluation of supervisors is an important component in the team management environment. Self-managing teams are the engines in the team management environment. Teamwork is most successful when the members are entrepreneurs who are willing to harness their abilities to the team's objectives.

The Power of Teams

In his book *Thriving on Chaos*, Thomas Peters contends that wholesale worker involvement must become a national priority if the United States is going to maintain, let alone improve, national economic well-being.[10] At the top of Peters's list is the use of teams. He exhorts managers to make self-managing teams the basic organizational building block. Peters contends that "the power of teams is so great that it is often wise to violate apparent common sense and force a team structure on almost anything." He urges readers to "empha-size mainly self-sufficient units, or what I call the small-within-big principle, throughout the organization."[11] Another of Peters's 45 prescriptions for U.S. business is to pursue what he calls "horizon-tal" management by bashing the bureaucracy. He suggests manag-ing the organization horizontally, insisting that vertical obfuscating be replaced with proactive, horizontal cooperation in pursuit of fast action.[12] The team management environment actively works toward that end.

Humanistic Values of Teamwork

Douglas McGregor asserts in *The Human Side of Enterprise* that teams can be effective:

> The face-to-face group is as significant a unit of organization as the individual. The two are not antithetical. In a genuinely effective group the individual finds some of his deepest satisfactions. Through teamwork and group activity many of the difficult organizational problems of coordination and control can be solved. However, these values can be realized only if certain requirements are met.[13]

McGregor explains how thinking must change in the team management environment:

> First, we will have to abandon the idea that individual and group values are necessarily opposed, that the latter can only be realized at the expense of the former. If we would look to the family, we might recognize the possibilities inherent in the opposite point of view.
>
> Second, we will have to give serious attention to the matter of acquiring understanding of the factors which determine the effectiveness of group action and to the acquisition of skill in utilizing their skills in group membership.
>
> Third, we will need to distinguish between those activities which are appropriate for groups and those that are not.
>
> Finally, we will need to distinguish between the team concept of management as a gimmick to be applied within the strategy of management by direction and control and the team concept as a natural correlate of management by integration and self-control. The one has nothing in common with the other.[14]

McGregor goes on to describe the benefits of teams:

1. Group target-setting offers advantages that cannot be achieved by individual target-setting alone. The two are sup-plementary, not mutually exclusive.

2. An effective managerial group provides the best possible environment for individual development. It is the natural place to broaden the manager's understanding of functions other than his own and to create a genuine appreciation for the need for collaboration. It is the best possible training ground for skill in problem solving and in social interaction.

3. Many significant objectives and measures of performance can be developed for the group that cannot be applied to the individual. The members of cohesive groups will work at least as hard to achieve group objectives as they will to achieve individual ones.

4. In an effective managerial team the aspects of "dog-eat-dog" competition, which are actually inimical to organizational accomplishment, can be minimized by the development of "unity of purpose" without reducing individual motivation.[15]

The team management environment is founded on McGregor's Theory Y, characterized as follows:

1. The expenditure of physical and mental effort in work is as natural as play or rest. The average human being does not inherently dislike work. Depending upon controllable conditions, work may be a source of satisfaction (and will be performed without threat of punishment).

2. Human beings will exercise self-direction and self-control in the service of objectives to which they are committed.

3. Commitment to objectives is a function of the rewards associated with their achievement.

4. The average human being learns, under proper conditions, not only to accept but to seek responsibility.

5. The capacity to exercise a relatively high degree of imagination, ingenuity, and creativity in the solution of organizational problems is widely distributed in the population.

6. Under the conditions of modern industrial life, the intellectual potentialities of the average human being are only partially utilized.[16]

Humanistic Management by Teamwork is founded on the principle that library employees are characterized by McGregor's Theory Y concept. Library employees can thrive in the team management environment, provided it is a well-managed system.

Well-Managed Systems

Rosabeth Moss Kanter describes the elements of well-managed systems in *The Change Masters: Innovations for Productivity in the American Corporation:*

> Participation would appear to work best when it is well managed. Well managed systems have these elements: a clearly assigned management structure and involvement of the appropriate line people; assignment of meaningful and manageable tasks with clear boundaries and parameters; a time frame, a set of accountability and reporting relationships, and standards that groups must meet; information and training for participants to help them make participation work effectively; a mechanism for involving all of those with a stake in the issue, to avoid the problems of power and to ensure for those who have input or interest a chance to get involved; a mechanism for providing visibility, recognition, and rewards for teams' efforts; and clearly understood processes for the formation of participative groups, their ending, and the transfer of the learning for them.[17]

It is instructive to examine Humanistic Management by Teamwork in light of Kanter's elements:

- *Clearly assigned management structure and involvement of the appropriate line people.*

The team management environment is readily defined by an organization chart that is more horizontal than vertical. Noticeably absent are layers between the dean and the departments of the library. Individuals in the team management environment know whom they report to in all instances. The department heads in the team management environment are directly involved in overall library management through the libraries management team.

- *Assignment of meaningful and manageable tasks with clear boundaries and parameters.*

The assignment and management of tasks within departments are left largely to the department heads. The assignment of tasks is dictated in large part by the approved job descriptions for staff and job assignments for librarians. Team meetings within departments offer ample opportunities for discussions of departmental objectives and reports on progress. The department head's role in the team management environment is less clear in terms of the boundaries and parameters. The administration delegates as much authority and responsibility as can be handled. Department heads become comfortable with their role in the team management environment through experience and trial and error.

- *A time frame, a set of accountability and reporting relationships, and standards that groups must meet.*

Accountability and reporting relationships in the team management environment are determined in large part by statements of job responsibilities and the performance-based evaluation system. Standards of performance are set and monitored within departments of the team management environment. Time frames for various activities are determined at the departmental level in keeping with library objectives and through discussions with other department heads and the dean.

- *Information and training for participants to help them make participation work effectively.*

Team members in the team management environment gain much of their information and training in team management through experience. The team leader has the primary responsibility for training in the team management environment and strives to make all members of the department active and effective team members.

- *A mechanism for involving all of those with a stake in the issue, to avoid the problems of power and to ensure for those who have input or interest a chance to get involved.*

The involvement of all staff in the team management environment is one of the greatest strengths of Humanistic Management by Teamwork. The library management team provides the opportunity for all department heads to become actively involved in library management and for the departmental teams to involve all persons in each department. Committees, task groups, the professional staff group, and the library faculty organization increase the opportunities for all who have input or interest to get involved in departmental and librarywide issues and initiatives.

- *A mechanism for providing visibility, recognition, and rewards for teams' efforts.*

The department heads in the team management environment are charged with the responsibility of providing for team visibility, recognition, and rewards. Visibility and recognition are provided through the library's internal newsletter and monthly departmental reports. The team gains visibility and recognition through individual participation in librarywide activities. Rewards are provided through the merit criteria guidelines for faculty and for department head recognition of meritorious staff during the annual salary-setting meeting of the library management team.

- *Clearly understood processes for the formation of participative groups, their ending, and the transfer of the learning for them.*

The library faculty organization and professional staff council have established bylaws that are readily available to anyone in the team management environment. Committees are established by the faculty's committee on committees, by the library management team, and by the dean. All committees and task groups begin with a formal charge, and all groups publish notes or minutes of their meetings, which are usually attached to the library's internal newsletter.

Humanistic Management by Teamwork

In September 1986, the University of New Mexico General Library (UNMGL) implemented a team management approach called Humanistic Management by Teamwork (HMBT). Robert L. Migneault described the approach in an article in *Library Administration & Management*.[18] The associate dean positions for technical services, collection development, and public services were eliminated, and a library administrative team composed of the dean, associate dean, and all directors and department heads was formed. Each of the 20 members of the library administrative team has all of the information needed to run the general library, including the entire operating budget and departmental reports. The team has responsibility for establishing programs, determining priorities, assigning responsibilities, and allocating resources. The dean's primary responsibilities are to provide leadership, represent the team to university administration, serve as convener of the team, and facilitate discussion. Team members work with, not for, the dean. As a direct result of Humanistic Management by Teamwork, high morale, self-esteem, and pride in the organization are evident throughout the library. The success of Humanistic Management by Teamwork at UNMGL can be attributed to the leadership of the dean and the commitment of all library faculty and staff to team management and to the library's goals.

Bibliography

American Management Association. *Participative Management*. New York: American Management Association, 1988.

Block, Peter. *The Empowered Manager: Positive Political Skills at Work.* San Francisco: Jossey-Bass, 1987.

Bookman, Robert. "Ignite Team Spirit in Tired Lions." *HRMagazine* (June 1990): 106–8.

Caouette, Wilfred G. *Participative Management and Psychology*. New York: Vantage Press, 1988.

Cox, Allan. "Everybody Wins with Teamwork." *Across the Board* (May 1990): 9–10.

Denton, D. Keith. "Effective Structures for the Management of Human Resources." *Australian Academic and Research Libraries* 16 (June 1985): 88–96.

—————. *Horizontal Management: Beyond Total Customer Satisfaction.* Lexington, Mass.: Lexington Books, 1991.

Drucker, Peter F. *Management: Tasks, Responsibilities, Practices.* New York: Harper & Row, 1974.

Gilberg, Jay. "Managerial Attitudes Toward Participative Management Programs: Myths and Reality." *Public Personnel Management* 17, no. 2 (summer 1988): 109–23.

Gilbert, G. Ronald. *Beyond Participative Management: Toward Total Employee Empowerment for Quality.* New York: Quorum Books, 1991.

Glassman, Edward. *For Presidents Only: Unlocking the Creative Potential of Your Management Team.* New York: Presidents Association, 1990.

Harris, Philip R. *Management in Transition: Transforming Managerial Practices and Organizational Strategies for a New Work Culture.* San Francisco: Jossey-Bass, 1985.

Isgar, Thomas. *The Ten Minute Team: Ten Steps to Building High Performing Teams.* Boulder, Colo.: Seluera Press, 1989.

Kanter, Rosabeth Moss. *The Change Masters: Innovations for Productivity in the American Corporation.* New York: Simon & Schuster, 1982.

—————. "The New Managerial Work." *Harvard Business Review* 67, no. 6 (November/December 1989): 85–92.

Kersell, J. E. "Team Management and Development in Montserrat and Anguilla." *Public Administration and Development* 10 (January 1990): 81–91.

Larson, Carl E., and Frank M. J. LaFasto. *Teamwork: What Must Go Right, What Can Go Wrong.* Newbury Park, Calif.: Sage Publications, 1989.

Maginn, Michael D. *Effective Teamwork.* Burr Ridge, Ill.: Business One-Irwin/Mirror Press, 1994.

McGregor, Douglas. *The Human Side of Enterprise.* New York: McGraw-Hill, 1960.

Michalko, James. "Management by Objectives and the Academic Library: A Critical Overview." *Library Quarterly* 45, no. 3 (July 1975): 235–52.

Migneault, Robert LaLiberte. "Humanistic Management by Teamwork in Academic Libraries." *Library Administration & Management* 2, no. 3 (June 1988): 132–36.

Monin, Gene. *Quality of Work Life, or, Participative Management.* Sault Ste. Marie, Ont.: Merlin, 1989.

Nadler, David A., and Michael L. Tushman. "Beyond the Charismatic Leader: Leadership and Organizational Change." *California Management Review* (winter 1990): 77–97.

O'Conner, Dee Dee. "Trouble in the American Workplace: The Team Player Concept Strikes Out." *Records Management Quarterly* (April 1990): 12–15.

Olivia, Lawrence M. *Partners Not Competitors: The Age of Teamwork and Technology.* Harrisburg, Pa.: Idea Group, 1992.

Ost, Edward J. "Team-Based Pay: New Wave Strategic Incentives." *Sloan Management Review* (spring 1990): 19–27.

Pardue, Howard M. "Is the Team on Your Side?" *Personnel Administrator* (November 1989): 64.

Peters, Thomas J. *Thriving on Chaos: Handbook for a Management Revolution.* New York: Alfred A. Knopf, 1987.

Plunkett, Lorne C. *High-Involvement Participative Management: Implementing Empowerment.* New York: John Wiley, 1991.

Priem, Richard L. "Top Management Team Group Factors, Consensus, and Firm Performance." *Strategic Management Journal* 11 (October 1990): 469–78.

Prince, George. "Recognizing Genuine Teamwork." *Supervisory Management* 34, no. 4 (April 1989): 25–31.

Rinke, Wolf J. "Empowering Your Team Members." *Supervisory Management* 34, no. 4 (April 1989): 21–24.

Scheuling, Eberhard E. "How to Build a Quality-Conscious Team." *Supervisory Management* 35, no. 10 (October 1990): 6–7.

Shonk, James H. *Working in Teams.* New York: AMACOM, 1982.

Stokes, Stewart L., Jr. "Building Effective Project Teams." *Journal of Information Systems Management* (summer 1990): 38–48.

Thamhain, Hans J. "Managing Technologically Innovative Team Efforts Toward New Product Success." *Journal of Product Innovation Management* 7 (March 1990): 5–18.

Veaner, Allen B. *Academic Librarianship in a Transformational Age: Program, Politics, and Personnel.* Boston: G. K. Hall, 1990.

Weiss, Donald H. "Effective Management of Effective Teams." *Supervisory Management* 35, no. 10 (October 1990): 10–11.

Notes

1. Allen Veaner, *Academic Librarianship in a Transformational Age: Program, Politics, and Personnel* (Boston: G. K. Hall, 1990), 447.

2. Ibid., 460.

3. Ibid., 447.

4. Peter F. Drucker, *Management: Tasks, Responsibilities, Practices* (New York: Harper & Row, 1974), 567.

5. Ibid., 568.

6. Ibid., 568.

7. Ibid., 569.

8. Ibid., 578.

9. Peter Block, *The Empowered Manager: Positive Political Skills at Work* (San Francisco: Jossey-Bass, 1987), 68–70.

10. Thomas J. Peters, *Thriving on Chaos: Handbook for a Management Revolution* (New York: Alfred A. Knopf, 1987), 297.

11. Ibid., 302.

12. Ibid., 459.

13. Douglas McGregor, *The Human Side of Enterprise* (New York: McGraw-Hill, 1960), 240.

14. Ibid., 240–41.

15. Ibid., 241–42.

16. Ibid., 247–48.

17. Rosabeth Moss Kanter, *The Change Masters: Innovations for Productivity in the American Corporation* (New York: Simon & Schuster, 1982), 275.

18. Robert LaLiberte Migneault, "Humanistic Management by Teamwork in Academic Libraries," *Library Administration & Management* 2, no. 3 (June 1988): 132–36.

•••••••Chapter 3

How Groups Work

"Nothing will ever be attempted,
if all possible objections must be first overcome."
—Samuel Johnson (1709–1784)

Methods of Organizing

The methods of organizing in today's academic libraries are governed by the characteristics of the people, the task to be performed, and the environment. All three of these factors have been changing in recent years and will continue to change rapidly in the future. Much of what can be seen in today's organizations is a carryover from past models of organization.

Industrial organizations, for decades, have been based on the breakdown of tasks. Large areas of responsibility were broken down into lesser responsibilities and assigned to specific jobs. These organizations were structured to perform well-defined tasks, with workers having predictable qualifications. Technological considerations were often more important than human considerations, and the gulf between what people were capable of doing and what they were required to do played little part in the design of the organizations. Specialization was thought to be the key to efficiency.

Specialization continues to be important. However, the breakdown of work into small segments and the relationships of the segments are changing because the nature of the work is changing. Work is becoming more complex, requiring more specialists to handle a narrower scope of work in greater depth. Rapid technological changes requiring specialization and problem solving in the more complex work environment have spawned an increasing variety of professional specialties. Common databases make it feasible to blend functions, until now quite separate, into innovative combinations.

The increasing complexity of work, the need for more specialization, and automation that has reduced the need for lower-skilled workers require that today's organizations examine alternatives to traditional patterns of organization. More coordination and integration are needed to improve the way groups work together. Organizations that in the past have been based on analysis are now being based, at least in part, on synthesis. Teams and work groups are being combined, often using members of different departments, to make a whole that is more effective than the individuals spread through several units.

Effective Groups

Knowledge of group behavior can be applied to improve the functioning of teams.[1] What distinguishes effective groups from those that are ineffective?

1. The effective group tends to be informal and relaxed. There are no obvious tensions; instead there is a comfortable atmosphere that can be observed after only a few minutes. It is a working atmosphere in which people are interested and involved, and there are no signs of boredom.

2. Nearly everyone participates in the discussions. If someone strays off the subject at hand, another member brings the discussion back on track.

3. Members of the team understand and accept the objective or task of the group. The objective has been discussed until it is formulated so that members can commit to it.

4. The members of the group listen to one another. Every idea is given a hearing, and members do not fear expressing their ideas.

5. There is disagreement. Team members are comfortable with conflict over ideas. Disagreements are not suppressed or covered up by premature group action. The group works to resolve disagreements rather than turning on the dissenter. Individuals who disagree are not attempting to dominate the group or be obstructive. Disagreements are genuine expressions of difference of opinion, and those opinions are given a hearing. The effective group deals with ideas and opinions, not personalities.

6. The effective team may have basic disagreements that cannot be resolved. The group accepts them and may elect to defer action to allow further study, or, if action is required, it will be taken with the understanding that the action may be subject to reconsideration at a later date.

7. The team makes decisions by consensus, in which everyone is in general agreement and willing to go along. There is little tendency for individuals who disagree with the decisions to keep their opposition private. Instead, those in disagreement are willing, once their positions are known, to go along. Formal voting is kept to a minimum and used only if consensus cannot be reached.

8. Criticism is frequent and relatively comfortable. There is little evidence of personal attack, either open or hidden. The criticism is constructive in that it is intended to remove obstacles that face the group and hinder its work.

9. Team members freely express their feelings and ideas on the problem at hand as well as on the performance of the team. There are few hidden agendas. Everyone appears to know how everyone else feels about any matter under discussion.

10. When decisions are made, it is clear who has responsibility for taking action.

11. The team leader does not dominate, nor does the team defer unduly to the leader. Leadership of the team shifts from one member to another, depending on the issue being discussed. This shift takes place because individuals on the team have different kinds of knowledge or expertise, and the team relies on individuals to take leadership on certain issues.

12. There appears to be no struggle for power in the effective team. It is not important who controls but that the job gets done.

13. The team performs maintenance on itself. If the team is not functioning properly or effectively, the problem or individual behavior interfering with group effectiveness will be openly discussed and a solution found before it proceeds.

14. In order for the team to be effective, a great deal of sensitivity, understanding, skill, and trust on the part of all members of the team are required.

Ineffective Groups

What are the characteristics of ineffective groups?

1. The atmosphere of the group is one of indifference and boredom, manifested in people whispering to one another or carrying on side conversations. There may be obvious tensions in the form of hostility, antagonism, or undue formality. The group is clearly not challenged or interested in its task.

2. A few members of the group dominate the discussion, and little is done to keep the discussion on track.

3. From observing the group's discussion, it is difficult to determine what its objectives are. The group may have a stated objective, but the members either do not understand or do not accept the objective. It is usually evident that individuals in the group have personal objectives that are in conflict with one another and with the group objective.

4. Members of the group do not really listen to one another, and ideas are either ignored or overridden. The discussion wanders from the task at hand, and individuals appear to be making speeches intended to impress rather than to further the group objective.

5. Members of the group fail to express their feelings or ideas for fear that other members will disagree or that the group leader is evaluating their contributions. Individuals are extremely careful about what they say.

6. The group does not effectively deal with disagreements. The leader may suppress dissension. Disagreements may result in open warfare between subgroups. Votes may resolve the issues at hand, but a small majority may be satisfied at the expense of the minority.

7. An aggressive individual or faction may dominate the majority of members, who wish to preserve the peace and get back to work. Less aggressive members are not heard.

8. Action is taken before sufficient discussion. Individuals who disliked the decision will complain after the meeting about not being able to voice their opinions. A simple majority vote is considered sufficient for action, and the minority remains resentful and uncommitted to the decision.

9. When decisions are made, it is unclear who will take action. Even when assignments are made, group members have doubts that action will be taken.

10. The chair is clearly the leader. Leadership does not pass to other members, regardless of their abilities.

11. Criticism often appears to involve personalities rather than issues. Members are uncomfortable with the criticism of ideas, because the criticism tends to be destructive rather than constructive. When every idea seems to get clobbered, the ideas stop coming out in discussions.

12. The general attitude about personal feelings is that they are explosive and should not be discussed. Therefore, personal feelings are hidden.

13. The group avoids discussion of its own operation. Instead, discussions about what went wrong and why generally take place outside the meetings.

14. Members of the group have low expectations of group accomplishment, partly because so many groups are ineffective.

15. Members of the group have little knowledge about effective group functioning and are fearful of conflict in group meetings.

Designing an Organization

How do you get flexibility into the organization and still maintain stability? How do you avoid too much time-consuming coordination and still take care of needed communication? The problem may be represented on a continuum. At one end are formality, structure, and control. On the other end are informality, free form, and creativity. The objective is to find a point on the continuum that achieves the right balance for the organization and its workers. Organizations that find themselves at one end or the other become either stifling or chaotic places to work, and the convenient middle yields mediocre results.

One approach is to have a system of organizations within the organization—a team organization. Team-based designs for organizations provide for a vertical focus on work through the existing structure and a lateral focus through teams. In some team-based organizations, work is accomplished through the voluntary collaboration of team members from various functional areas. The four types of teamwork models are work groups, task teams, matrix organizations, and project organizations. The four types may be used in any combination. The possibilities are numerous.

Work Groups

The work group or department team is a group of individuals within a department who have an unusual amount of autonomy and authority to handle a given task. They are normally allowed to plan their own work and set their own work rules, based on goals set by or negotiated with the supervisor. Normally work groups are long-standing, and membership in them is full-time.

Task Teams

Task teams are assembled from various departments to work together for a considerable period of time to achieve specific goals. Although individuals are expected to give their full attention to the task at hand, their primary responsibilities are to the home department. Often, task teams are assembled to launch a new program or solve a particular problem. The task teams are similar to committees in organizations.

Matrix Organizations

In the most advanced of team-based designs, the matrix organization, both vertical and lateral lines carry formal authority. The matrix organization is the superimposition of a project over the functional organization. People on the team have two bosses, the project leader and their home department supervisor. An individual in the matrix might have two or more bosses, an obvious, yet intentional violation of the principle of unity of command. The individuals on the assembled team are carefully selected for their expertise.

Project Organizations

A project organization is an organization carved out of the functional organization. It is designed to achieve a specific purpose and retains only a loose connection with the functional organization in that it has little obligation to coordinate its work. Members of the project organization are often not guaranteed employment when the project is completed. An example of such an organization is a grant-funded project or a retrospective conversion project.

Quality Circles

Another use of teams in organizations is the quality circle. Quality circles originated in Japan and are a type of production committee. As used in the United States, quality circles deal with a broader range of activities than just quality. The groups are intent on solving problems and discovering improved methods of production. For example, the installation of quality circles at Northrop Corporation was based on the following philosophy:

1. People want to participate.
2. People basically want to do a good job.
3. Workers are individuals with brains that should be used.
4. Each worker has unlimited, untapped capacity.
5. Every worker knows best what is keeping them from doing a good job.

6. Each worker is an expert on their job, and this expertise should be recognized and deferred to.

7. The company needs each person's help and respects each person's judgment.

8. Workers as a team can make the company a better place to work.

Northrop's quality circles are composed of 10 to 12 people from the same work area, who meet voluntarily to solve problems in their areas. After formation, the group goes through eight one-hour training sessions on problem solving. Cost-saving innovations result in monetary rewards that go into the quality circle's account, which may then be spent by the group in accordance with company guidelines.

Total Quality Management

Total Quality Management (TQM) focuses on "doing the right thing the first time."[2] It involves quality teams whose focus is on teamwork and processes rather than on individual efforts and tasks. TQM requires careful planning, listening to the customer, teamwork, and involvement of everyone in the process. It also requires special training, systematic searching for ways to improve, measuring performance, and an esprit de corps that comes from people in the organization feeling appreciated. All of these factors build on each other and are guided by a shared vision and what is needed to achieve it.

One way that TQM differs from quality circles is that the emphasis is on management. Not only must quality improvements be managed, the quality teams must have the support of management. If you attempt to make quality improvements in isolation, it is unlikely that the improvements will be long lasting, because too many things can undercut them. Unless there is a supportive administration, there is no assurance that changes will be continued if things go wrong or if you leave. To be successfully implemented, TQM requires not only the vision and leadership of top management but also the resources for implementation of quality improvements in the organization.

Many organizations that have implemented TQM have conducted organizational assessments to identify those processes to be targeted for change and to provide a baseline measurement for judging progress. The following questions are often used as the basis for assessment:

- What is the mission of the organization? What products and services are offered?

- Who are the internal and external customers?

- What measurement systems are presently in place?

- Does the organization measure its success in terms of meeting customer requirements and expectations?

- How well does the organization communicate with its customers and its suppliers?

- How much emphasis is placed on planning as opposed to fire fighting?

- How does the organization generate ideas for improvement? Improvement in general or quality improvement specifically?

- What type of suggestion system is in place? How effective is it?

- What does the organization reward? Improvement in general or quality improvement specifically?

- To what extent is teamwork used, encouraged, and recognized?

- What is the nature of management's relationship with employee unions?

- How well do functional units cooperate? Are turf battles endemic?

- Does the executive leadership have credibility in the eyes of middle and line managers? Frontline workers?

- What type of management style is employed? Is it directive or participative?

- How much discretion do employees have in making decisions? Is authority delegated to the lowest levels possible?

- What is the attitude toward training?

- What is the attitude toward quality work? Is the focus on quality of the end product or quality of the process?

- Are the organization's values, goals, objectives, policies, and procedures clearly stated and widely known?

- Does the organization have an abundance of priorities or have a vital few been identified and articulated?

We will not attempt to thoroughly explain TQM but suggest that you read one or more of the many excellent books on the subject listed in the bibliography. TQM in the team management library has a high likelihood of success, given the teamwork and participative management already in place.

Team Requirements

A team is not characterized by free form or the absence of regimentation. The team must have a continuing mission and clearly defined objectives.

Team design requires a continuing mission in which the specific tasks change frequently. If there is no continuing mission, there might be a need for an ad hoc temporary task force but not an organization based on the team as a permanent design. If the tasks do not change, or if their relative importance or sequence remains unchanged, there is no need for team organization and no point to it.

Without clearly defined objectives, the team will drift from one activity to the next, devoting its efforts to nonproductive goals. The team must help define objectives, but the team leader must see that there are objectives. It is not "top" leadership's responsibility to always make the decision and give the command. It is leadership's responsibility to decide who among the team members has responsibility for a particular phase or challenge. A team is therefore not democratic, if by that is meant that decisions are taken by vote. It emphasizes authority, but the authority is task-derived and task-focused.

It is always the team as a whole that is responsible for the task. The individuals contribute their particular skills and knowledge. But every individual is always responsible for the output and performance of the entire team rather than for his or her own work.[3] The team is the unit.

In *Management: Tasks, Responsibilities, Practices*, Peter Drucker describes how to operate teams for top management work, which is work for a team rather than for one person:

1. Whoever has primary responsibility in a given area has, in effect, the final say. No subordinate can appeal a decision by one member of the team to another member. Every member speaks with the full authority of top management.

2. No member will make a decision with regard to a matter for which he or she does not have primary responsibility. It is a wise precaution for members of the top management team not even to have an opinion on matters that are not within their own areas of primary responsibility.

3. Members of the top management team need not like each other. They need not even respect each other. But they must not agitate against each other in public.

4. A top management team is not a committee. It is a team. The team leader is not the boss, that person is a leader.

5. Within their assigned sphere, a member of top management is expected to make decisions. But certain decisions should be reserved for the team.

6. The top management task requires systematic and intensive work on communications among the members.[4]

At UNMGL, Humanistic Management by Teamwork departs from the principles of top management teams in two important ways. First, all members of the library's top management team contribute to team decisions, and the individual with primary responsibility in a given area follows the group's consensus decisions. Second, members of the library management team do have to respect each other. Humanistic Management by Teamwork is grounded in respect. Only persons who have the respect of their colleagues are appointed to serve on the library's management team.

Member Requirements

People are put on teams because of their authority, knowledge, and motivation. The crucial qualifications for team membership are knowledge and authority. Members must bring their knowledge to bear on the team, and where expertise is needed, it must be available to the team. All members of a team should have or be given authority to make decisions that are consistent with those of other members of the team and with those of the team.

Team members need not know each other well to perform as a team. But they do need to know each other's function and potential contributions. Mutual understanding of each other's job and understanding of the common task are essential.

Some managers believe that all employees prefer a job that requires interaction with others and that everyone wants more autonomy. Not everyone wants to interact with a group. There are highly motivated and productive people who are ill equipped to function on a team or simply not interested in functioning on a team or in a team environment. Their contributions are as individuals, and those individual contributions should be recognized and valued by the organization.

In order for any team to be effective, members must be motivated to work with others; they must bring their knowledge to the team; they must collectively have the needed authority to make decisions; and the team membership must be changed as the situation or goal of the team changes. A note of caution: There is a point at which coordination can be carried too far. When people begin to feel that they are spending a disproportionate amount of their time mechanically coordinating their efforts with the work of others, you should be concerned about the design or activity of the organization.

Individuals who aspire to participate in an organization based on teamwork would do well to assess their own abilities in regard to positive teamwork behaviors. The following statements, answered affirmatively, indicate an aptitude for success as a team member or team leader: [5]

- I cooperate with my colleagues.

- I collaborate, whenever possible, with people from other disciplines, departments, and work units.

- I seek input from diverse sources for problem solving and decision making.

- I recognize the interdependence of technical and service staff with others within and outside of the library.

- I can function effectively as a member of a team or task force.

- I am willing to consider issues from varied perspectives, even those that are very different from mine.

- I can tolerate ambiguity.

- I can tolerate uncertainty.

- I can tolerate a seeming lack of structure.

- I take an interest in each co-worker's achievements.

- I take an interest in the organization's achievements.

- I am able to give and receive feedback in an objective, nondefensive manner.

- I encourage an atmosphere that is informal, relaxed, comfortable, and nonjudgmental.

- I seek group participation, consensus, and shared decisions.

- I clarify roles, relationships, responsibilities, and expectations.

- I have the capacity for establishing temporary, meaningful, and intense relations.

- I can facilitate group communication on objectives, goals, and missions.

- I can synthesize diverse input, information, and insights.

- I encourage authentic communication, enabling employees to speak freely and express feelings.

- I emphasize the constructive channeling of energy caused by disagreements and differences.

- I seek group support, recognition, and encouragement for individual employees.

- I attempt to draw everyone into discussions, even the silent and insecure.

- I share the leadership role by fostering others to initiate, clarify, summarize, and decide.

- I model ethical behavior to others.

Pitfalls in Team Structures

Instituting team management is not without its pitfalls. The top management of the organization must take into consideration a number of factors and realities before deciding to implement a team-based organization.

Do not ignore the fact that attitudes may be a problem. Middle management must be as willing to change as top management, and that may take time. Unions may be reluctant to accept changes that give employees more autonomy. If employees feel that the organization is encouraging them to express their ideas, it might make them question the value of union representation. The groundwork for change to a team management environment must be laid in order to alleviate distrust of management. The solution is to actively invite and encourage participation to make participation voluntary, and to assure employees that their jobs will be secure.

Do not ignore middle management. It must be prepared to change. One of the greatest pitfalls in introducing team management is that middle managers are hesitant to relinquish to subordinates what they believe is their decision-making prerogative. They not only must share decision making with teams but also must share information with others to a greater extent than normally has been the case. The established department heads may see the change as degrading to their self-images. It is obvious that if the perceptions of managers do not change, infighting will result.

Do not hesitate to call in outside help. Changes in organizations will be more readily accepted if employees know that their top management is on solid ground with its plan for change. Training sessions on team building can be conducted by consultants brought in for that purpose.

Do not sacrifice a logical structure for a behavioral theory. Base your organizational design on a viable structure. The notion that individuals will achieve higher levels of satisfaction by eliminating all rules and structure is precarious thinking. Individuals and groups need some structure and guidance. Take care that you do not abandon well-defined responsibilities and channels of communication.

Do not allow teams to become seperately independent. Teams are part of the larger organization and must serve its goals. Communication must be maintained both horizontally between teams and vertically between teams and higher management.

Do not let the new system become rigid. Just when you think the organization is perfectly aligned, it is time to think about changes that must be made because the tasks and challenges to the organization are changing. Top management must also be cautioned that too many changes are disruptive and can easily result in inefficiency. The top management team has a responsibility to monitor the organization's work and its goals to ensure that teams throughout the organization have not become rigid.

Do not assume that training is a onetime thing. A training program needs to accompany changes that radically alter worker responsibilities. Training must continue in order to maintain the skills and knowledge of team members and to improve understanding of the team management environment.

Do not assume that teams do not need to be managed. The team management environment focuses work on results, and it enlarges the scope of responsibility of individuals. The team organization will not, however, replace the need for performing traditional tasks in traditional ways. Each team must understand its goals and its decision-making processes. There must be ground rules, and the team leader has an extremely important role. Control is essential in the team management environment. An eye must be kept on the bottom line and on project timetables. The tendency to "let George do it" in the team management environment is a real danger. The team leader has a responsibility to ensure that the "it's everybody's responsibility and no one's" mentality does not pervade the team management environment.

Do not underestimate people. When individuals are given a larger sense of responsibility and opportunity, they will usually rise to the occasion. If the work is important to individuals, it is hoped that their sense of dedication and responsibility will rise accordingly, manifested, for instance, in reduced absenteeism and apathetic behavior.

Do not overestimate people. Given the freedom to manage themselves to a greater degree, some individuals will take advantage of you and the system. Absenteeism may in fact increase for some employees. The team management environment encourages cross-departmental teams and, as a result, multiple bosses at times. Some individuals cannot cope and become distressed over the ambiguities inherent in the team management environment. If these problems cannot be overcome, these individuals should be excluded from task groups. Some individuals are incapable of planning their own work, do not wish to have more autonomy or responsibility, or do not wish to participate in team activities. A few individuals would prefer to sabotage a system in which others are succeeding. All of these individuals, if proven they will not or cannot participate, should be excluded from critical team operations.

Do not believe that results will be immediate. There is often a time lag of seven to 18 months between a change in leadership behavior and improved performance. In addition, it requires from six to 12 months for top management to be able to change leadership behavior down through the organization. Therefore, it can be expected that it will take more than a year for a major management change in the organization to lead to the desired effect.

Five kinds of inequalities can drive a wedge between individuals and the team: [6]

1. The seductiveness of the hierarchy. Teams that are pulled together from different departments, with the awareness that they will be returning to them, may slip into deference patterns that give those with higher status more authority in the group. So teams may end up duplicating the organization hierarchy in miniature inside the team.

2. The knowledge gap. Participants are made, not born. It takes knowledge and information to effectively contribute to group tasks. Persons in some positions have greater access to information than other members of the team. The knowledge gap needs to be closed before team meetings in order for all to participate.

3. Differing personal resources. Members of the team have various levels of participation skills, including verbal skills. There are often coalitions within groups wherein individuals support one another. Skills such as those involved in articulating opinions, developing arguments, and reaching decisions differ among members.

4. The seniority or activity gap. Newcomers or outsiders often feel uncomfortable about speaking up. The group may have developed its own language, acronyms, and understandings that are not obvious to newcomers and that may inhibit participation.

5. Internal politics. The team may also develop factions and subgroups that inhibit group progress.

Bibliography

Barlow, Richard. *Team Librarianship: The Advent of Public Library Team Structures.* London: Library Association, 1989.

Barry, D. "Managing the Bossless Team: Lessons in Distributed Leadership." *Organizational Dynamics* (summer 1991): 31–47.

Benne, K., and P. Sheats. "Functional Roles of Group Members." *Journal of Social Issues* (1948): 2, 42–47.

Blanchard, K., et al. *Leadership and the One Minute Manager.* New York: William Morrow, 1985.

Carew, D., et al. *The One Minute Manager Builds High Performing Teams.* San Diego, Calif.: Blanchard Training and Development, 1990.

Cargill, Jennifer, and Gisela M. Webb. *Managing Libraries in Transition.* Phoenix, Ariz.: Oryx Press, 1987.

Celebrating Excellence. *Quality, Service, Teamwork and the Quest for Excellence: The Keys to Business Success in the 90's.* Lombard, Ill.: Celebrating Excellence, 1992.

Chaudhry-Lawton, Rani. *Quality: Change Through Teamwork.* London: Century Business, 1992.

Davis, Stanley M., and Paul R. Lawrence. *Matrix.* Reading, Mass.: Addison-Wesley, 1977.

Doyle, Robert J. *GainManagement: A Process for Building Teamwork, Productivity & Profitability Throughout Your Organization.* New York: American Management Association, 1992.

Drucker, Peter F. "Effective Structures for the Management of Human Resources." *Australian Academic and Research Libraries* 16 (June 1985): 88–96.

Dyer, W. G. *Team Building: Issues and Alternatives.* Reading, Mass.: Addison-Wesley, 1987.

Fordyce, Jack K., and Raymond Weil. *Managing with People: A Manager's Handbook of Organization Development Methods.* Reading, Mass.: Addison-Wesley, 1979.

Galbraith, Jay R. *Designing Complex Organizations.* Reading, Mass.: Addison-Wesley, 1973.

Glaser, Rollin, and Christine Glaser. *Building a Winning Management Team.* Bryn Mawr, Pa.: Organization Design and Development, 1986.

Guest, Robert H. *Work Teams and Team Building*. Elmsford, N.Y.: Pergamon Press, 1986.

Hannan, Geoff. *Collective Management: Teamwork*. Hemel Hempstead, England: Simon & Schuster Education, 1992.

Hastings, Colin, et al. *The Superteam Solution: Successful Teamworking in Organizations*. San Diego, Calif.: University Associates, 1987.

Herbert, Theodore T., and Ralph W. Estes. "Improving Executive Decisions by Formalizing Dissent: The Corporate Devil's Advocate." *Academy of Management Review* 2, no. 4 (October 1977): 662–67.

Howard, Helen. "Organization Theory and Its Applications to Research in Librarianship." *Library Trends* 32, no. 4 (spring 1984): 477–93.

Kanter, Rosabeth Moss. "From Status to Contribution: Some Organizational Implications of the Changing Basis for Pay." *Personnel* 64, no. 1 (January 1987): 12–37.

Lacoursiere, R. B. *The Life Cycle of Groups*. New York: Human Science Press, 1980.

Lawrence, Paul R., and Jay W. Lorsch. "New Management Job: The Integrator." *Harvard Business Review* 45, no. 6 (November/December 1967): 142–51.

———. *Organization and Environment: Managing Differentiation and Integration*. Rev. ed. Boston: Harvard Business School Press, 1986.

Lewis, David W. "An Organizational Paradigm for Effective Academic Libraries." *College & Research Libraries* 47, no. 4 (July 1986): 337–53.

Lowell, Gerald R., and Maureen Sullivan. "Self-Management in Technical Services: The Yale Experience." *Library Administration & Management* 4, no. 1 (winter 1990): 20–23.

Maier, Norman R. F. "Assets and Liabilities in Group Problem Solving: The Need for an Integrative Function." *Psychological Review* 74 (1967): 239–49.

Manz, Charles C., and Henry P. Sims, Jr. "Leading Workers to Lead Themselves: The External Leadership of Self-Managing Work Teams." *Administrative Science Quarterly* 32, no. 1 (March 1987): 106–29.

———. "Super Leadership: Beyond the Myth of Heroic Leadership." *Organizational Dynamics* (spring 1991): 18–35.

Martell, Charles R. *The Client-Centered Academic Library: An Organizational Model.* Westport, Conn.: Greenwood, 1983.

Martin, Lowell A. *Organizational Structure of Libraries.* Library Administration Series, 5. Metuchen, N.J.: Scarecrow Press, 1984.

Mason, Richard O. "A Dialectical Approach to Strategic Planning." *Management Science* 15, no. 3 (March 1969): 408.

Matejko, Alexander J. *In Search of New Organizational Paradigms.* New York: Praeger, 1986.

McCabe, Gerard B. "Contemporary Trends in Academic Library Administration and Organization." In *Issues in Academic Librarianship: Views and Case Studies for the 1980s and 1990s,* edited by Peter Spyers-Duran and Thomas V. Mann, Jr., 21–35. Westport, Conn.: Greenwood, 1985.

Metcalf, Keyes D. "Departmental Organization in Libraries." In *Current Issues in Library Administration,* edited by Carlton B. Joeckel, 90–110. Chicago: University of Chicago, 1939.

Miles, Robert H. *Macro Organizational Behavior.* Santa Monica, Calif.: Goodyear, 1980.

Mintzberg, Henry. *The Structuring of Organizations.* Englewood Cliffs, N.J.: Prentice-Hall, 1979.

Mohrman, Susan Albers, and Thomas G. Cummings. *Self-Designing Organizations: Learning How to Create High Performance.* Reading, Mass.: Addison-Wesley, 1989.

Mussman, K. "Socio-technical Theory and Job Design in Libraries." *College & Research Libraries* 39, no. 1 (January 1978): 20–28.

Prince, George. *The Practice of Creativity.* New York: Collier, 1970.

Reddy, W. Brendan, ed. *Team Building: Blueprints for Productivity and Satisfaction.* San Diego, Calif.: University Associates, 1988.

Ricking, Myrl, and Robert E. Booth. *Personnel Utilization in Libraries: A Systems Approach.* Chicago: American Library Association, 1974.

Riggs, Donald E., and Gordon A. Sabine. *Libraries in the '90's: What the Leaders Expect.* Phoenix, Ariz.: Oryx Press, 1988.

Robey, Daniel. *Designing Organizations: A Macro Perspective.* Homewood, Ill.: Richard W. Irwin, 1982.

Schein, Edgar H. *Organizational Culture and Leadership.* San Francisco: Jossey-Bass, 1985.

Stokes, Stewart L., Jr. "Building Effective Project Teams." *Journal of Information Systems Management* (summer 1990): 38–58.

Sundel, M., et al. *Individual Change Through Small Groups*. New York: New American Library, 1985.

Troy, Kathryn. *Employee Buy-In to Total Quality*. New York: Conference Board, 1991.

Tunley, Malcolm. *Library Structures and Staffing Systems*. London: Library Association, 1979.

U.S. Department of Energy. *Guide to Good Practices for Teamwork Training and Diagnostic Skills Development*. Washington, D.C.: U.S. Department of Energy, 1982.

U.S. Office of Personnel Management, Federal Quality Institute. *Federal Total Quality Management*. Washington, D.C.: U.S. Government Printing Office, 1990.

Van de Ven, Andrew H. *Group Decision Making and Effectiveness: An Experimental Study*. Kent, Ohio: Kent State University Press, 1974.

Waddell, William D. *Overcoming Murphy's Law*. New York: AMACOM, 1981.

Weick, Karl. *The Social Psychology of Organizing*. 2d ed. Reading, Mass.: Addison-Wesley, 1977.

Wellins, Richard, and Jill George. "The Key to Self-Directed Teams." *Training & Development Journal* (April 1991): 26–31.

Notes

1. Douglas McGregor, *The Human Side of Enterprise* (New York: McGraw-Hill, 1960), 240–41.

2. James H. Saylor, *TQM Field Manual* (New York: McGraw-Hill, 1992), 10.

3. Peter F. Drucker, *Management: Tasks, Responsibilities, Practices* (New York: Harper & Row, 1974), 556.

4. Ibid., 622–24.

5. Philip R Harris, "Team Synergy Analysis Inventory," in *Management in Transition* (San Francisco: Jossey-Bass, 1985), 357–59.

6. Rosabeth Moss Kanter, *The Change Masters: Innovations for Productivity in the American Corporation* (New York: Simon & Schuster, 1982), 256.

•••••••••Chapter 4

Authority and Management
in the Teamwork Library

"A man is not necessarily intelligent because
he has plenty of ideas, any more than
he is a good general because he has plenty of soldiers."
—Chamfort (1741–1794)

How Is the Team Management Library Organized?

The team management library is organized in the traditional manner of departments that have units within departments. The primary difference lies in to whom those heads of departments report. In the traditional hierarchy, department heads report to associate deans or directors for public services, technical services, or collections, for example. In the team management environment, the department heads report directly to the dean, eliminating the traditional associate and/or assistant dean or director levels. The elimination of the associate/assistant dean or director levels places all members of the organization one level closer to the top of the organization chart.

The authority normally associated with the associate/assistant dean or director levels positions is now in the hands of department heads, who must exercise greater authority without trampling on the authority of fellow department heads or the dean. That exercise of authority requires that decisions be made on the departmental level when they do not affect other departments, or that decisions be made in partnership with other departments. The library management team provides the formal opportunity for information sharing as well as shared decision making. The traditional associate/assistant dean or director levels tend to artificially separate or compartmentalize the public, technical, and collections departments. The elimination of the higher levels requires that department heads work together on shared concerns. As a result of shared decision making by department heads, the staff within respective departments also have more contact with one another, and the barriers disappear between collection development, technical, and public services.

Five Functions of Management in the Team Management Environment

Every person in every academic library organization manages, is managed, or is affected by management. The traditional functions of management are the foundation for every person with supervisory responsibilities in the team management environment. The set of activities carried out by all of these persons includes planning, organizing, staffing, leading and motivating, and controlling:

- The planning function includes determining the mission, goals and objectives, and direction of a unit and developing strategies for achieving them.

- Organizing involves creating a structure for accomplishing tasks, including assigning work.

- Staffing is the process of selecting, training, evaluating, disciplining, and rewarding staff.

- By creating a climate in which employees accomplish work, supervisors provide leadership and motivation for employees.

- Controlling is the process by which supervisors determine if and how well the unit is accomplishing its goals.

Authority in the Team Management Environment

One of the most important concepts in the team management environment is authority. Authority is the permission needed to carry out responsibilities. It is handed down from the top, beginning with the highest levels. Those who appoint the governing body of the institution, by virtue of the appointment, provide that body with authority to manage the institution. Authority for the operation of the institution is delegated to the university president, who delegates authority to the appropriate vice president, who delegates certain authority to the dean or director of the library. As authority is passed down the line to the library, that authority becomes more specific. The dean or director has the authority to manage the library's budget and operations. Department heads, unit heads, and individual supervisors are given the authority needed to manage programs and supervise employees with specific jobs and work to perform.

In the team management environment, authority is delegated for many of the programs and operations and is shared by all who participate in the library's top management team. If the dean does not share authority with department heads and others, the team management environment will surely dissipate.

Team leaders and members of the management team must have a sense for how much authority they are free to exercise and when they need to consult others. It is not always possible to spell out precisely what authority should be delegated or shared. It may, in fact, vary by individual, according to how much each can manage. Conversely, the dean must be careful to avoid delegating more authority to one branch head than to another branch head, provided both are equally capable. In the team management environment, team leaders or department heads throughout the library system may have authority to approve expenditures up to a given amount; otherwise, the top library management team must be consulted.

Authority in the team management environment needs to be shared as much as possible among and between teams throughout the library system and among and between individual team members. To an outside observer, it may be more difficult to determine where authority lies in the team management environment than in a hierarchy. One will note that department heads, unit heads, and members of teams all have authority to some degree. Decisions are made at lower levels and by groups of persons far more often in the team management environment than in a hierarchy. Nevertheless, final authority still lies with the dean. We will examine how the team management library is viewed by other parts of the university in a later chapter.

Sources of Authority

Three sources of authority as viewed by team members are legal, competence, and referent power. Team leaders and members of the top library management team have legal authority by virtue of their positions. Humanistic managers use legal authority sparingly in the team management environment. Others in the departmental or unit teams know who has legal authority and do not want or need to be told, "Do this because I am the department head." That authority does exist, however, if it must be used.

Authority based on competence is the most effective. Competence refers to the knowledge, abilities, and skills held by the individual who is department head or team leader. The acceptance of competence as a source of authority is especially important when one is working with other library faculty and professional staff in a department or unit.

Similarly, members of the team are more inclined to accept leadership if their team leader has referent power. This is authority derived from experience, seniority, or status in librarianship. One who is respected for professional accomplishments and publications, or who is highly regarded by other department heads and team leaders, will be more readily accepted by team members.

Exerting Authority

The humanistic team leader needs to know how to exercise authority and to feel comfortable doing it. Managers in the team management environment are most effective when they rely little on their legal authority. Power derived from competence and referent authority works best in teamwork. Team leaders must have a good feel for what authority they have and do not have. This knowledge must be gained through experience and working with other team leaders and the administration. Team leaders are careful not to flaunt their authority but to share it with the team. Authority is delegated to get the job done, not to show who is the boss. Always, when exercising authority, good team leaders are considerate of others and try to promote team spirit. Humanistic managers prefer to use persuasion instead of exerting their authority. In addition to the authority given by the organization, team leaders are more successful when they have one or more of the following: job knowledge, trustworthiness, and ability to persuade.

Delegating Authority

Generally, organizations have three classifications of authority by which supervisors can make decisions: complete authority (take action without consulting), limited authority (take action but supervisor must be informed), no authority (may not take action without checking with supervisor). In order to accomplish departmental objectives, it is necessary to delegate responsibility and authority to team members. Remember that the two—responsibility and authority—go together. In delegating, one must make it clear what authority is being delegated and at what level.

Leadership in the Team Management Environment

Leadership is an essential requirement for good team management. There are many definitions of leadership, as evidenced by the number of books on the subject. Leadership in the context of Humanistic Management by Teamwork is simply the ability to elicit desired behavior without necessarily evoking authority or power. It is a knack that may be developed with hard work or may come naturally. Successful leaders possess the following qualities: a belief in their ability to lead, a sense of mission, the willingness to put the organization's well-being above their own egos, honesty, courage, sincerity, dependability, job knowledge, common sense, sound judgment, energy, and the willingness to work hard.

There are three basic kinds of leadership. Autocratic leadership is a technique whereby the leader makes the decisions and demands that employees follow instructions without question. Democratic leadership involves those being supervised; the leader consults with employees and lets them help set policy. With free-rein or participative leadership, the leader exercises minimum control, allowing workers to use their own judgment and sense of responsibility to accomplish the necessary work.

Different kinds of leadership can be successful with different employees. An autocratic style works best in a situation in which the supervisor has real authority and a personality that can exert strong control. Participatory or democratic leadership works best in situations in which the supervisor's authority is not clearly defined, the procedures are subject to change with the situation, and employees are required to use creativity and initiative.

Participative or free-rein leadership is most effective in the team management environment. In the team management library, employees are expected to cooperate, to be self-reliant, and to exercise their own judgment. Team leaders are responsible for setting good examples for employees to adopt and follow. In the team management environment, the top library management team sets the example for the organization. It must be composed of members who not only possess leadership qualities but also work to develop leaders in teams throughout the library system, especially in their given areas of managerial influence. The success of the team management library depends on it.

Decision Making

Without question, the ability to make decisions is a valuable attribute for any library organization. This is especially true in the team management environment, where it is possible for important decisions to be postponed because of interminable discussions or lack of understanding about who will make the decision.

When making decisions, the supervisor exhibits leadership skills while providing assurance to employees that everything is under control. The skill of making decisions under pressure must be developed in order for a supervisor to be effective. The same must be said about the top library management team that faces unique difficulties. Not only must decisions be reached with reasonable speed, but decisions must be understood by all team members, and the persons responsible for communicating and implementing the decisions must be identified.

In order to be decisive, team members must want to solve problems and must have the confidence to do so. Good decision makers must know how and when to make decisions and must be aware of the factors that influence those decisions. Most important, the team must have information with which to make good decisions. One of the primary advantages of management by teamwork is that most of the individuals who have relevant information for decision making are present at meetings. For example, the top management team at the

University of New Mexico General Library invites all interested parties within the library to participate in decision discussions.

Giving Direction

The successful team leader is able to provide leadership to the team without being obvious about it. It used to be assumed that all a supervisor had to do was order an employee to do something and the employee would do it. This attitude in the team management environment will not work. Today's library employees deserve more consideration. If members of the team are given some say in decisions that affect them, they will work harder as a result.

Good supervision in the team management environment is the art of getting others to do what you want, when you want it, and how you want it. In order to succeed as a team leader, you must humanistically elicit cooperation. You have to be able to develop good relations with those you supervise and earn their cooperation. The following are some ways to practice good supervision:

- Stress team effort whenever possible.

- Reward people who do more than you ask of them.

- Set realistic goals with the help of team members.

- Praise team members.

- Never criticize an employee in front of others.

- Supervise with persuasion, not force or pressure.

- Support and help members of the team when they need and request it.

- Be honest about problems and issues with the team, and involve them in problem solving and decision making.

Motivation

All library organizations want and need motivated employees. There will normally be highly motivated individuals and self-starters who wish to work in the library, and some of them will work in your library. In the real world and in the team management environment there are also unmotivated librarians and staff who contribute to low morale, absenteeism, and high turnover. Employee motivation, for the purposes of this discussion, is defined as those techniques that influence the actions of individuals to help them integrate personal needs and goals with those of the organization.

Employees' motivational drives and societal attitudes toward work affect their motivation. For this reason, the team management environment can inhibit or contribute to individual motivation, but motivation is primarily self-generated. Nevertheless, job satisfaction and motivation are closely tied. Those things that individuals do not like about their work are usually factors such as an unpleasant environment, long hours, poor working conditions, low pay, lack of advancement opportunity, or poor supervision, rather than the nature of the job itself. What individuals do like about jobs are those aspects that provide challenge, responsibility, variety, recognition, meaning, satisfaction, and reward.

The job itself can be a motivator to employees. The team management environment offers employees at the lowest levels of the traditional hierarchical structure the opportunity to participate fully as team members. The team leader has a responsibility to provide everyone in the team with challenges, recognition, and meaning.

Coaching

Coaching is akin to continuous training. Just as an athletic coach provides the knowledge and skill training for athletic competition, the team leader has the responsibility for not only training but also keeping up the skills and knowledge that employees require for the job. As members of the team begin to slip away from the basic skills that made them productive, coaching is needed. Among the reasons for slippage in a person's skills is boredom. Regular coaching is one of the best ways to combat the negative effects of boredom and get employees back on the right track. Team leaders must be aware that individual performance affects team performance, and, for the team to succeed, each individual must succeed. Coaching one-on-one is the most effective means for changing individual behavior.

The team leader must be able to identify the behavior that needs changing and know the behavior that is desired. Coaching is teaching and guiding, not scolding or preaching. Here is a logical step-by-step process:

1. Observe the present behavior, compare it with the ideal behavior, and identify what must be changed.

2. Discuss the needed changes with the employee.

3. Get the employee to talk about ideas for improving the task.

4. Demonstrate the desired behavior until the employee can do it correctly and can explain the reason for doing it that way.

5. Praise the employee for correct behavior.

A good team leader coaches in much the same manner that a good football coach coaches a team. Corrective measures are taken when a change is needed in an observable behavior. Coaching is an excellent way to alter behavior, making a good employee an excellent employee. It is a continual process that is an extension of training in the team management environment.

Counseling

Counseling has a more personal aspect to it than does coaching. Coaching is intended to improve a person's job skills, whereas counseling is a private discussion of problems that have a bearing on job performance. When something is worrying the employee, the team leader must discover it and correct it if possible.

There are two types of counseling sessions: those initiated by the team leader and those initiated by a member of the team. Both are equally important, and the team leader must be available whether the purpose is to discuss a personal problem or to allow the employee to "blow off steam." In a counseling session initiated by the team leader, the purpose is often to address performance. The situation is quite different when the employee asks to meet with the team leader. The team leader may only be needed as a sounding board for the employee, someone to talk to about a personal problem. It is important that team leaders know their limitations in this situation. Psychologists have the proper training to counsel employees with emotional problems.

Team leaders in the team management environment have a responsibility to help team members grow in their chosen fields. The temptation is great to keep an outstanding team member in the department when, in fact, that person is prepared to move on in the organization or beyond. Team leaders who are in a position to help team members advance should do so by serving as references or encouraging individuals to explore other opportunities, without appearing to be eager to get rid of good team members. The team leader makes it a habit to counsel or mentor employees on a regular basis.

Bibliography

Bass, Bernard M. *Leadership and Performance Beyond Expectations.* New York: Free Press, 1985.

Bennis, Warren G., and Burt Nanus. *Leaders: The Strategies for Taking Charge.* New York: Harper & Row, 1985.

Bensimon, Estela Mara. *Redesigning Collegiate Leadership: Teams and Teamwork in Higher Education.* Baltimore, Md.: Johns Hopkins University Press, 1993.

Bittel, Lester R. *What Every Supervisor Should Know.* New York: McGraw-Hill, 1980.

Broadwell, Martin M. *Moving up to Supervision*. 2d ed. New York: John Wiley, 1986.

———. *Supervising Today: A Guide for Positive Leadership*. 2d ed. New York: John Wiley, 1986.

Broadwell, Martin M., and Ruth Sizemore House. *Supervising Technical and Professional People*. New York: John Wiley, 1986.

Cargill, Jennifer, and Gisela M. Webb. *Managing Libraries in Transition*. Phoenix, Ariz.: Oryx Press, 1987.

Daughtrey, Anne Scott, and Betty Roper Ricks. *Contemporary Supervision: Managing People and Technology*. New York: McGraw-Hill, 1988.

Drucker, Peter F. "Effective Structures for the Management of Human Resources." *Australian Academic and Research Libraries* 16 (June 1985): 88–96.

Fallon, William K., ed. *Leadership on the Job: Guides to Good Supervision*. New York: AMACOM, 1981.

Fisher, Kimball. *Leading Self-Directed Teams: A Guide to Developing New Team Leadership Skills*. New York: McGraw-Hill, 1993.

Hawkins, Katherine W. "Implementing Team Management in the Modern Library." *Library Administration & Management* 3, no. 1 (winter 1989): 11–15.

Hersey, Paul. *The Situational Leader*. New York: Warner Books, 1984.

Hodgetts, Richard M. *Effective Supervision: A Practical Approach*. New York: McGraw-Hill, 1987.

Howard, Helen. "Organization Theory and Its Applications to Research in Librarianship." *Library Trends* 32, no. 4 (spring 1984): 477–93.

Howell, J., et al. "Substitutes for Leadership: Effective Alternatives to Ineffective Leadership." *Organizational Dynamics* (summer 1990): 21–38.

Howell, Jane Mary. *Charismatic Leadership: Effects of Leadership Style and Group Productivity on Individual Adjustment and Performance*. Vancouver, B.C.: University of British Columbia, 1986.

Kanter, Rosabeth Moss. "From Status to Contribution: Some Organizational Implications of the Changing Basis for Pay." *Personnel* 64, no. 1 (January 1987): 12–37.

Klingner, Donald E. "When the Traditional Job Description Is Not Enough." *Personnel Journal* 58 (April 1979): 243–48.

Kouzes, James M., and Barry Z. Posner. *The Leadership Challenge*. San Francisco: Jossey-Bass, 1987.

Lawrence, Paul R., and Jay W. Lorsch. *Organization and Environment: Managing Differentiation and Integration*. Rev. ed. Boston: Harvard Business School Press, 1986.

Lewis, David W. "An Organizational Paradigm for Effective Academic Libraries." *College & Research Libraries* 47, no. 4 (July 1986): 337–53.

Loden, Marilyn. *Feminine Leadership or How to Succeed in Business Without Being One of the Boys*. New York: Times Books, 1985.

Martell, Charles R. *The Client-Centered Academic Library: An Organizational Model*. Westport, Conn.: Greenwood, 1983.

Martin, Lowell A. *Organizational Structure of Libraries*. Library Administration Series, 5. Metuchen, N.J.: Scarecrow Press, 1984.

McCabe, Gerard B. "Contemporary Trends in Academic Library Administration and Organization." In *Issues in Academic Librarianship: Views and Case Studies for the 1980's and 1990's*, edited by Peter Spyers-Duran and Thomas W. Mann, Jr., 21–35. Westport, Conn.: Greenwood, 1985.

Metcalf, Keyes D. "Departmental Organization in Libraries." In *Current Issues in Library Administration*, edited by Carlton B. Joeckel, 90–110. Chicago: University of Chicago, 1939.

Migneault, Robert LaLiberte. "Humanistic Management by Teamwork in Academic Libraries." *Library Administration & Management* 2, no. 3 (June 1988): 132–36.

Mussman, K. "Socio-technical Theory and Job Design in Libraries." *College & Research Libraries* 39, no. 1 (January 1978): 20–28.

Ricking, Myrl, and Robert E. Booth. *Personnel Utilization in Libraries: A Systems Approach*. Chicago: American Library Association, 1974.

Siegel, Laurence, and Irving M. Lane. *Personnel and Organizational Psychology*. 2d ed. Homewood, Ill.: Richard W. Irwin, 1987.

Tjosvold, Dean, and Mary M. Tjosvold. *Leading the Team Organization*. New York: Lexington Books, 1991.

Tunley, Malcolm. *Library Structures and Staffing Systems*. London: Library Association, 1979.

Yukl, Gary A. *Leadership in Organizations*. Englewood Cliffs, N.J.: Prentice-Hall, 1981.

•••••••Chapter 5

Implementing Team Management in Academic Libraries

"I don't want any yesmen around me.
I want everyone to tell me the truth
—even though it costs him his job."
—Samuel Goldwyn (1882–1974)

Planning for Change

Prerequisites for Implementing Team Management

Team management requires rethinking the entire organizational structure, especially if the existing structure represents traditional hierarchy. The dean or director of the library must be committed to team management in both word and deed. Top administrators must trust and have the trust of library faculty and staff. They must be willing and able to delegate authority and responsibility throughout the organization.

Teamwork requires a strong commitment of all administrators, managers, and supervisors in the library organization. Gone will be the days when a select group of three to seven library administrators made all the major decisions for the library. To be effective, team management requires the redistribution of decision making in the organization. Associate and assistant deans or directors will be required to rethink their traditional roles. One model suggests that they should be placed in staff rather than line positions, eliminating one layer of administration and making department heads directly responsible to the dean.

Once authority and responsibility have been delegated, department heads play a critical role in library-wide team management. Their ability to accept and exercise authority will determine in large part whether team management will succeed or fail. Parochial and protection-of-turf attitudes and activities must give way to concern for broader, library-wide issues and actions.

The following are ideal conditions for implementation of team management in libraries:

1. The dean or director is committed to changing the traditional or hierarchical organization and is committed to the sharing of authority.

2. The associate and assistant deans or directors are committed to changing the organization, or there are vacancies in those positions.

3. A high level of trust exists between library administration and department heads and staff.

4. A level of trust and harmony exists between librarians and staff.

5. The organization is accepting of change.

6. All concerned have or will gain a complete understanding of what teamwork involves and requires of library faculty, administrators, and staff.

Preparing for Change

Let's assume that the director has determined that the library should change to team management in order to make the most of the potential that exists when employees work as teams. In preparing for change, the director must gather information about how successful changes have been in the past. Has the library experimented with the team structure before, and if so, what happened? The director must make clear what the expectations are and communicate clearly how team management will change the workplace. It is also essential to make clear whose idea it is to change the organization and to present a case for the need for change. The director must develop support and allies among higher management and middle managers, specifying how the team management environment fits into the overall organization. It might be prudent to consider first implementing the change at a certain level in the organization or in one accepting unit or branch.

Change is the planned or unplanned response of an organization to pressures. Change also involves an attitude or a state of mind. For our purposes, change will be planned in response to the need for a library that maximizes the potential that exists when employees are assembled as groups or work teams.

The attitudes of the director or some managers in the library may complicate the change to management by teamwork. Three specific leadership types may cause difficulties: the visionary, the technocrat, and the sympathizer. The visionary may make sweeping changes without thoroughly considering the consequences or even planning for change. Although vision is critical, it needs structure.

The technocrat tends to focus only on outcomes, without consideration of the individuals who must implement the changes. The sympathetic leader leans too far the other way. Sympathetic leaders devote too much attention to individuals' feelings about change, which can kill momentum. After a while, employees want and need leadership and guidance, not just understanding. Granted, these three types are extremes, but they can be found among library managers. Any of these can inhibit planning for change.

Five Key Tasks in Successful Implementation of Change

To implement change as a planned, orderly process, the leader must consider how to motivate people to change, how to obtain the right resources for change, and how to make the change work. The library director must perform five key tasks before and during the implementation of organizational change. The director must clarify plans, integrate new practices, provide training, foster ownership, and provide information and receive feedback.

It is essential that plans be well developed and carefully considered prior to implementation. The development of plans should be the product of input from appropriate individuals and groups and should have the support of the opinion leaders in the library. Make certain that there are clear objectives and defined outcomes. Plans must be carefully communicated, highlighting primary benefits to library personnel and to the constituents served by the library. Make sure that the plans are distributed to the right personnel to gain support.

Change should be introduced in steps, if possible. The first step in Humanistic Management by Teamwork is to establish the top library management team and begin team-building activities. Care should be taken to publicize each change step, not only what is being changed but also the rationale for change.

The library director must provide support for training in team building as an integral part of the implementation process. Beginning with top management, there must be commitment to the idea that team building as a strategy for change is more effective than trying to rely solely on a one-to-one supervisor-employee relationship. Also, both supervisors and employees must feel the need to change the traditional ways of working together. Training should be an ongoing process during the life of the team management organization.

In addition to planning, changing practices, and providing training, the library director must empower the library faculty and staff to make change happen. When they understand and participate in team management, they will become committed to the new system. The library director must make the employees feel that team management is personally beneficial to them. The talents and skills of every library employee must be used through skillful delegation by the library director. Collaboration with employees on how changes can be made to improve the overall operation of the library is an excellent way of fostering ownership of change.

The library director needs feedback from library faculty and staff to determine the impact of the change and to gauge its success. The director who makes giving and getting feedback a habit will find that employees will be more open with comments, opinions, and ideas. Directors must also act on suggested ideas, to the limit possible. Progress and problems need to be shared with everyone possible throughout the entire organization in order to generate team spirit and commitment to library-wide goals.

An Assessment of Team Leadership Abilities

In order for the team management concept to succeed, the director must make a candid assessment of the people who will play a leadership role in the change from a hierarchical organization to the team management environment. Library directors must understand the roles they will play and which roles can be delegated to others. This activity requires honest self-assessment as well as the skillful assessment of others. The following types should be identified among library faculty and staff:

- Inventor: Integrates trends and information into concepts, models, and plans; envisions the big picture and adapts plans.

- Entrepreneur: Instinctively focuses on organizational efficiency and effectiveness; identifies critical issues and new possibilities; actively seeks advantages and opportunities.

- Integrator: Forges alliances; gains personal acceptance as well as team acceptance; relates practical plans to strategic plans and organizational issues.

- Expert: Takes responsibility for the technical knowledge and skills required; uses information skillfully and explains it in a logical way.

- Manager: Simplifies, delegates, assigns priorities; develops others; gets the job done at all costs.

- Sponsor: Ensures support and resources for the highest level of the organization; communicates where the changes fit in the overall organizational vision.

One person in the library's management team may fulfill more than one role, and there may be several persons performing the same role. For change to succeed, the behaviors or skills for each of the roles must be represented by members of the management team.

Implementation of HMBT

When Humanistic Management by Teamwork (HMBT) was introduced at the University of New Mexico General Library (UNMGL), it replaced a hierarchical system that had been in place for many years. When the dean initiated HMBT, the faculty and staff welcomed the change. Because it was implemented from the top down, the first persons affected were department heads, who had to balance their roles as department heads and as members of the library management team. Resistance to the change was minimal during the first years and lessened as new employees were hired into an existing team management environment. The most difficult part of implementing HMBT was convincing library faculty and staff that the dean was serious about sharing authority. Individuals throughout the organization became convinced over time through the dean's words, and more important, his actions.

An assessment of the nature of a given organization and of the library faculty and staff that make up the organization's lifeblood is essential prior to attempting team management in a large library. Team management may not be for all library organizations, nor for all library employees, including the dean or director, or library department heads. Library employees must be professionally motivated and appreciate professional camaraderie. Library managers and supervisors must have basic professional respect for their colleagues. Team management is not for people who are insecure, or who cannot properly handle their insecurities.

The implementation and everyday maintenance of team management is not easy. To talk about team management as an idea and to espouse its virtues in principle are relatively easy. Once the change is implemented, keeping a team honed for professional action is, of course, something else. Not to diminish the roles and impact of all participating parties, if the library dean or director is eager, willing, and able to remain steadfast in orchestrating team management, team management can succeed remarkably. Keeping a large team of self-directed, diverse, and professionally aggressive managers on a collectively constructive path is outright hard, tiring work. Assuming productive orchestration, the leader in a team management setting must devote attention to each member of the team as an individual. There will always be disappointments and frustrations for participants. When all is said and done, institutional gains and managerial accomplishments that come with team management will prevail over temporary thoughts of giving it up for a less complicated managerial arrangement.

When the idea of team management was first introduced at UNMGL, the parties immediately involved were ready for a change—a change in library organization, in library governance, and in the way of conducting business. Most of the persons immediately involved could only gain authority and enhance their individual capacity for influence. Not inconsequentially, team management was introduced with the guarantee that it could be abandoned after one year for a different managerial arrangement. Members of the top library management team voted after the first year to keep team management intact. Team management also was introduced with the understanding that two vacant assistant dean positions would be eliminated. A search in progress to fill one of the vacant positions was canceled in favor of the less hierarchical team management structure. During the life of team management, there has been some resistance over the specifics of membership. Some people resisted the admission of certain individuals to the top library management team or resisted adding members. The resistance has been handled with patience and by allowing individuals time to get accustomed to the proposed changes.

How can team management be implemented throughout the organization? Should it be implemented? In principle, if team management is implemented as the primary means by which the library is managed, team management must be implemented throughout the library as the method of choice. Managers throughout the library organization are responsible for implementing team management. Reality has it that not all managers want to engage in team management. Not all managers are capable of engaging successfully in team management. Given that team management predominates in the library, its positive influence will eventually persuade and ultimately endure.

Critics sometimes charge that team management is not cost-effective. The criticism emanates from the general observation that so many people gather together to deliberate on matters that could be handled by fewer people. Relatively speaking, team management that is calamitous will not be as cost-effective as an efficient hierarchical organization. However, team management at its best can be extremely cost-effective, especially when implementing major changes in the organization. Team management at its best facilitates the exchange of ideas, informed deliberation, and communication for meeting organizational goals and objectives. The question of cost-effectiveness must be considered in the context of value-added dimensions.

Humanistic Management by Teamwork can be implemented in both large and small libraries. Assuming the presence of professionally prepared people, team management can be successfully implemented in virtually any size library. Nevertheless, the larger the library, the more complex the group dynamics are likely to be. The size of the library notwithstanding, team management requires a leader who advocates team management and a complement of managers and supervisors who value professionalism, professional camaraderie, diversity, compromise for institutional excellence, and decision making by consensus.

HMBT cannot be implemented without ample preparation. An institution contemplating this change must accept that it will take time to see major and lasting positive results, say, three to five years. Assuming the given institution and employees are professionally prepared and willing to give team management a chance, the best place to begin is to establish a top library management team that includes all department heads and above. Every member of this team has line responsibility directly to the library dean or library director. Then, the HMBT process evolves one step at a time.

Mistakes Commonly Made in Implementing Change

1. Failure to take the end user into account.
2. Failure to recognize all of the functions involved in the change.
3. Failure to delegate responsibilities.
4. Failure to recognize who will be affected.
5. Failure to develop an influence strategy to get support for change.
6. The tendency to consider only short-term costs.
7. The tendency not to define expectations clearly.
8. The tendency to ignore complaints instead of considering their possible legitimacy.

Putting Teams Together

There are many ways to implement teams in organizations and no right way for everyone. The experience at the University of New Mexico General Library may be useful for libraries considering team management. Chapter 11 includes a description of how HMBT was implemented there in 1986.

Team Management as a Continuum

The team approach to management represents a dynamic, always changing system. All groups go through changes as they grow from a collection of individuals to a functioning team. As individuals join or leave the team, the team changes. Team effectiveness is affected by how long members have been participating and how far members have advanced in their development. Differences from one team meeting to the next are noticeable when certain members are absent or replaced by substitutes.

In a hierarchy, if the boss is consistent, everyone knows what to expect from the beginning. In a team management environment, the team must be nurtured and given time to develop. Changes occur more frequently in the team management environment because of changes in membership and because the team moves back and forth between stages of development, perhaps never reaching its maximum potential or reaching it for only brief periods. Experience shows that a team that has been working together for several months will have a series of very effective meetings and then lapse into a relatively unproductive period. The team leader must be patient. The temptation is great, when the team is functioning poorly, to abolish team management and revert to a hierarchical organization.

On a continuum, team management lies between hierarchy and anarchy, incorporating features of both the hierarchy and participative management. The variations are noticeable among and even within departments of the team management library. Those departments depending heavily on the performance of staff doing routine tasks will naturally lean toward the hierarchical approach. Turnover in staff is greater, leading to more difficulties in team building, and staff at that level normally need more direction. At the other end of the continuum are departments with the highest-level staffing and lower turnover, employees who are willing and able to fully participate as team members. Within a department, the team leader may move back and forth between the roles of leader of the team and boss, depending on how well the team is performing. The best approach lies in consistency, which is somewhere in the middle of the continuum. The team will and should expect the team leader to exert authority when needed and also to encourage participation as much as possible.

Participative Management

Participative management encourages involvement of employees in decision making on library operations. True participative management encourages employees to share their thinking and opinions of the work and how it should be performed. Participative management, as practiced in the library, offers the following benefits:

1. It gives people the right to be creative members of a cooperating group. Library faculty and staff serve together on numerous committees.

2. It leads to new relationships between employee and supervisor and between employees. It also encourages horizontal communication among departments of the library.

3. It can spur less skilled employees to greater effort, and it encourages them to accept responsibility. The attitude of cooperation among library employees is contagious.

4. It usually results in greater job satisfaction and output of employees. Morale in the library is higher when employees have a stake in the organization.

5. It enables employees to accept change more easily, because they have participated in deciding the extent of change and how it should be implemented.

The library that adopts Humanistic Management by Teamwork will use participative management, especially as it relates to the involvement of staff in decision making.

Stages of Team Development

The One Minute Manager Builds High Performing Teams describes the following stages of development for teams: orientation, dissatisfaction, resolution, and production.

- Group Development Stage 1—Orientation characteristics include the following:[1]
    - Feeling moderately eager with high expectations
    - Feeling some anxiety
    - Testing the situation and central figures
    - Depending on authority and hierarchy
    - Needing to find a pace and establish oneself
- Group Development Stage 2—Dissatisfaction characteristics include the following:[2]
    - Experiencing a discrepancy between hopes and reality
    - Feeling frustrated
    - Reacting negatively toward leaders and other members
    - Competing for power and attention or both
    - Experiencing polarities: dependence/counterdependence
- Group Development Stage 3—Resolution characteristics include the following:[3]
    - Decreasing dissatisfaction
    - Resolving discrepancies between expectations and reality
    - Resolving polarities and animosities
    - Developing harmony, trust, support, and respect

- Being more open and giving more feedback
- Sharing responsibility and control
- Using team language
- Group Development Stage 4—Production characteristics include the following:[4]
    - Feeling excited about participating in team activities
    - Working collaboratively and interdependently with whole group and subgroups
    - Feeling team strength
    - Showing high confidence in accomplishing tasks
    - Sharing leadership
    - Feeling positive about task successes
    - Performing at high levels

The authors of *The One Minute Manger Builds High Performing Teams* offer many helpful and useful methods for team building. The old-fashioned approach, akin to football coaching, assumes that the individuals on the team need skill development, direction, and goals. However, the successful team requires that all members come to the situation with some level of knowledge, skills, desire, and motivation. All realize that the team functions only as well as does each individual. Natural leaders come to the fore and assume their roles. The work ethic is assumed, and the poor performers are quickly identified. It is important to remember, however, that few individuals are natural team members. The following three sections provide suggestions on how individuals can improve their participation in teams and how teams can be most effective.

How to Improve Participation in Groups

Philip Harris, in *Management in Transition*, gives the following suggestions for how individuals can improve their participation in teams:[5]

- Be experimental. Test new styles of leadership and communication, different kinds of behavior and attitudes, new patterns of personal participation and relationships.

- Be authentic. Be honest in team communications and avoid game playing with each other; care about team members enough to confront them when necessary and tell them like it is.

- Be sensitive. Express your own feelings, and be conscious of others' feelings. Respond empathetically and reflect on the sender's real meaning in message exchanges. Be aware of a whole range of nonverbal communications and cues.

- Be spontaneous. Respond creatively to here-and-now data produced in the group, especially to personal revelations of self. Not only confirm others in their sharings, but also avoid being manipulative.

- Be helpful. Accept others' perceptions of themselves, of others, and of situations as being valid whether you agree or not, and avoid imposing your opinions, values, and systems on others. Unless others perceive your intervention as helpful, it is not. Others must be aided to discover new dimensions through you.

- Be open and flexible. Consider other viewpoints, alternatives, and possibilities, rather than being closed-minded or locked into previous positions. Be adaptable, not rigid, in responding to innovative ideas or perceptions of differences.

- Be time conscious. The group has limited time together and schedules to keep, so limit personal inputs and avoid dominating team communications or diverting the group from its mission. Cultivate conciseness, preciseness, and listening skills, while bringing the wayward back on target.

- Be a group leader. Share distinctive competencies and permit others to make their unique contributions to team talk and maintenance functions. Team participation is an opportunity to practice a range of leadership skills, whether as initiator or follower.

Eight Characteristics of Effective Teams

Larson and LaFasto identify the following eight characteristics or properties of effectively functioning teams:[6]

1. A clear, elevating goal. An effective team must have a clear understanding of its goals and must consider the goals worthwhile and important. The goals should be personally challenging and elevating in the sense that they are important. Team members must believe that accomplishment of the goals will make a difference.

2. A results-driven structure. The design and structure of the team must be appropriate for the goals of the team. The structure must make sense to the members and must not confuse effort with results. The effective team has clear roles and responsibilities, an effective communication system, methods for evaluating performance, and objective and factual information for decision making.

3. Competent members. Effective teams must have members who possess the necessary technical skills and knowledge and who have personal characteristics required to achieve excellence while working well with others. Team members must also have a strong desire to contribute and the ability and desire to collaborate with others.

4. Unified commitment. Effective team members must have a sense of loyalty and commitment to the team. Unified commitment involves a dedication and enthusiasm for the team's goals and an intense identification with a group of people.

5. A collaborative climate. Effective teams thrive in an environment of trust. This environment is characterized by honesty, openness, consistent and predictable behavior, and respect. Trust allows team members to stay focused on the problem at hand, promotes effective communication, and improves the quality of collaborative work.

6. Standards of excellence. Effective teams establish and meet standards of excellence in terms of performance, individual commitment, motivation, and self-esteem. Performance standards are formally established and evaluated, but commitment, motivation, and self-esteem seldom are. They are established informally, sometimes unconsciously, and play a role in performance evaluation. Individual team members need to require one another to sustain standards of excellence. The team also needs to exert pressure on itself to establish and sustain standards and not rest on its laurels.

7. External support and recognition. The absence of external support and recognition is quite noticeable in poorly functioning teams, and its presence is a sign that the team is successful. The team is given the resources it needs to perform and is supported by others outside the team.

8. Effective leadership. Effective leaders establish a vision of the future, create change, and unleash the talents and energy of team members. Effective leaders influence others to move from the status quo toward a vision of the way things should be. Effective leaders have a plan for change and demonstrate to team members that change is not only possible, it is positive. Effective leaders also motivate team members to take action by generating enthusiasm and commitment to the team's objectives.

Positive Behaviors and Attitudes of Team Members

Research at the East-West Center in Honolulu, reported by Moran and Harris in 1982, indicates that the following behaviors and attitudes of team members contributed to team success:[7]

1. Tolerance of ambiguity

2. Tolerance of uncertainty

3. Tolerance of a seeming lack of structure

4. Interest in the group's achievements

5. Interest in each individual's achievements

6. Ability to give and accept feedback in a nondefensive manner

7. Openness to change

8. Openness to innovation

9. Openness to creative, joint problem solving

10. Ability to create a team atmosphere that is informal

11. Ability to create a team atmosphere that is relaxed

12. Ability to create a team atmosphere that is comfortable

13. Ability to create a team atmosphere that is nonjudgmental

14. Capacity to establish intense, short-term member relations

15. Desire to encourage group participation

16. Desire to encourage group consensus

17. Desire to encourage group decisions

18. Appreciation of effective listening and communication that serve group needs and that stay on target and on schedule

19. Capacity to cultivate a team spirit of constructive criticism and authentic, nonevaluative feedback

20. Group attitude that invites members to express feelings

21. Group attitude that invites members to be concerned about group morale and maintenance factors

22. Clarification of member roles, relationships, assignments, and responsibilities

23. Shared leadership so as to fully utilize all member resources

24. Periodic reexamination of maintenance functions that affect team progress and communication

25. Fostering of trust within the group

26. Fostering of confidence within the group

27. Fostering of commitment within the group

28. Sensitivity to the team's linking functions with other working groups

29. Promotion of group norms so that members are respectful and supportive of one another and realistic in mutual expectations

30. Use of approaches that are goal directed, that divide labor fairly among members, and that synchronize efforts

31. Providing for team-building opportunities in the midst of completing tasks

Team Leaders in Team Management

Individuals in the team management environment with supervisory or management responsibilities are considered team leaders, although their titles are normally department head, director, or unit head, or specific titles such as acquisitions librarian or archivist. In addition to their abilities as team leaders, it is important that they be humanistic in their approach to management. A supervisor who is a disciplinarian or authoritarian will have difficulties, because it is incumbent upon team leaders to get others to work with them rather than for them. All of the talk about teamwork will fall on the deaf ears of employees if the team leader does not practice what is preached. The next section deals with identifying individuals for team leader positions.

Identifying Prospective Team Leaders

Team leaders may be chosen on the basis of seniority, proficiency, favoritism, demonstrated leadership, experience, or educational background. It is not unusual and is often desirable to select someone from the staff for a supervisory position. Making the transition to a supervisory position requires a great deal of effort on the part of the employee as well as psychological, social, and educational support from management.

Persons who will become good team leaders can be identified quite easily from among existing library personnel. Those individuals will be highly skilled at their jobs, have good communication skills, get along well with co-workers and management, and have a positive attitude. All the attributes of a good employee are needed to become a good team leader. Above all, prospective team leaders must like their work, other people, and themselves.

The team management environment stresses good communication skills and humanistic management abilities. The individual who cannot communicate well will experience tough sledding in the team management environment. A strict disciplinarian or one who is not self-motivated will have difficulty getting team members to work together. One attribute that is seldom considered is a sense of humor. The team management environment requires extensive interaction with others, and one must not take oneself too seriously.

Personal Qualities of Good Team Leaders

What are the personal qualities of good team management environment supervisors?

1. Energy and good health. Supervision is a demanding activity and requires that individuals not only perform a variety of activities but also be physically and emotionally up to the task.

2. Leadership potential. Supervisory responsibilities in the team management environment require the ability to get people to work for and with you to accomplish the objectives of your unit.

3. Ability to get along with people. One of the most important qualities management looks for in a team leader is the ability to get along with others. Members' feelings toward their team leader greatly influence how well they carry out their responsibilities.

4. Job know-how and technical competence. The team leader must know the job in order to be effective in training and problem solving. Team leaders usually have their own job duties and responsibilities in addition to supervision and must be proficient in those duties.

5. Initiative. Team leaders need to be able to recognize when adjustments must be made in the work flow or changes made in order to improve procedures. They must also be capable of recognizing when the team is not functioning well. Initiative is required in order to be aware when potential problems loom.

6. Dedication and dependability. Workers who sense that their team leader is not dedicated to the job, the employer, or the team often mirror that attitude. The example set by the team leader will be followed by team members.

7. Positive attitude toward team management. An uncommitted team leader will have an uncommitted team.

These characteristics are desirable in any employee but are most important in those in supervisory positions on the team. If your team leaders do not exhibit all of these positive attributes, training and staff development can be provided to enhance these characteristics.

Team Leader Attitudes

Attitude is extremely important to good supervision in any library organization, and especially in the team management environment. Team leaders have the proper attitude if they agree with the following statements:

1. Team leaders must manage with a high degree of integrity and lead by example.

2. Team leaders must keep their word to employees.

3. Team leaders must earn the respect, trust, and confidence of employees.

4. Team leaders must strive to help employees develop to their full potential.

5. Team leaders must give credit to employees who do a good job.

6. Team leaders must accept team and higher-level management decisions and directives and support them.

7. Team leaders must not discuss personal feelings about management with employees but should discuss disagreements privately with management.

8. Team leaders must be responsible for the performance of their employees and the team.

9. Team leaders must be objective in judging the actions of employees.

10. Team leaders must decide matters involving employees on the basis of facts and circumstances, not on personal sympathies.

11. Team leaders must accept the responsibility for rehabilitating rather than punishing employees whenever possible.

12. Team leaders must be prepared to support employees in cases where employees are in the right.

13. Team leaders must allow employees to have as much control over their own work as possible.

14. Team leaders must work to maintain a climate in the work-place that allows employees to express their feelings and concerns openly without fear of reprisal.

See chapter 9 for further discussion of the supervisory role.

Who Should Not Be a Team Leader?

There are types of persons to avoid when filling supervisory positions in the team management environment. If selecting a person from the present staff, avoid these persons: the negative, the unmotivated, the rigid, the unproductive, and the disgruntled employees. The attitude of a negative employee will be contagious among team members, and the unmotivated employee will not have the initiative to lead the team. The rigid employee will be unable to effectively deal with constant change. The unproductive employee will find it difficult to get others to work as a team, and the employee who is unhappy with the work, team management, the department head, the organization, or life in general will not be able to take on the challenges of the team management environment.

All managers think first of their best workers when supervisory positions become available. The best worker, however, is not necessarily the best supervisor in the team management environment. Selecting the best worker to be a team leader is a common and possibly dangerous practice. Because of the money, prestige, or status, good workers often accept supervisory positions without realizing that the skills required of a good worker are not the same as those required of an effective team leader. Because they do not develop the necessary supervisory skills, they perform poorly. If they do not enjoy the work, some quit. Others may receive poor evaluations, possibly leading to termination. Others may stay in supervisory positions they dislike because they do not want to lose face.

Persons should go into supervisory positions because they want the challenge and satisfaction to be gained. If these are not the reasons for seeking supervisory responsibility in the team management environment, no amount of pay, prestige, or status will compensate for the stress and other problems associated with the position.

In selecting a team leader, you must look for someone who has good communication skills, likes people, has the aptitude for the work, and has energy and enthusiasm. A person with these attributes has a high likelihood of being a successful team leader in the team management environment.

The HMBT Library Environment

The prevailing climate of the Humanistic Management by Team-work library is characterized by professional camaraderie; one could call it managerial camaraderie. A team management environment facilitates self-imposed standards, the result of which is relatively high morale throughout the work-place. Self-imposed standards enrich one's professional integrity. This, coupled with high morale, yields high productivity, outstanding service, and ongoing renewal in the areas of librarianship, scholarship, and research, as applicable.

Trust is an important ingredient in the team management library. The degree of effectiveness of team management very much depends on the level of trust among the team management group. The essence of team building is trust building. The team management environment necessitates the testing of the trust factor from time to time. If the trust quotient is judged to be relatively low, something has to be done to improve the situation. Otherwise, team management cannot really work.

Delegation is also quite important. One of the primary principles on which team management is built is delegation according to people's knowledge, competencies, or strengths. Where one person may be relatively strong, another may be relatively weak. Team management flourishes when the complement of collective strengths is greater than the sum of its parts.

The most rewarding aspects of the team management environment are the give and take of professional camaraderie and the productive results thereof, for example, ongoing professional and managerial renewal. The baser aspects of human nature and the vicissitudes of life in general are the greatest problems with management by teamwork. Pettiness sometimes creeps in, and individual bickering over turf stifles team management. Individuals are expected to excel while integrating their initiative into the group culture. Without the right kind of leadership, team management quickly dissipates.

Bibliography

Benne, K., and P. Sheats. "Functional Roles of Group Members." *Journal of Social Issues* 4, no. 2 (spring 1948): 2, 42–47.

Blanchard, K., et al. *Leadership and the One Minute Manager*. New York: William Morrow, 1985.

Bradford, Leland, ed. *Group Development*. San Diego, Calif.: University Associates, 1979.

Byham, William C., and Jeff Cox. *Zapp! The Lightning of Empowerment: How to Improve Productivity, Quality, and Employee Satisfaction*. New York: Harmony Books, 1990.

Carew, D., et al. *Fundamentals of Effective Teamwork.* San Diego, Calif.: Blanchard Training and Development, 1990.

———. *Group Development Stage Analysis.* San Diego, Calif.: Blanchard Training and Development, 1990.

———. *Group Observation Form.* San Diego, Calif.: Blanchard Training and Development, 1990.

———. *The One Minute Manager Builds High Performing Teams.* San Diego, Calif.: Blanchard Training and Development, 1990.

———. *Situational Leadership II and Stages of Group Development.* San Diego, Calif.: Blanchard Training and Development, 1990.

Cohen, A. M., and R. D. Smith. *The Critical Incident in Growth Groups: Theory and Technique.* Reading, Mass.: Addison-Wesley, 1976.

Dimock, H. *Groups: Leadership and Group Development.* San Diego, Calif.: University Associates, 1987.

Drucker, Peter F. "The Coming of the New Organization." *Harvard Business Review* 66, no. 1 (January/February 1988): 45–53.

Dyer, W. G. *Team Building: Issues and Alternatives.* Reading, Mass.: Addison-Wesley, 1987.

Forsyth, D. *An Introduction to Group Dynamics.* Monterey, Calif.: Brooks/Cole, 1983.

Gatto, Rex P. *Teamwork Through Flexible Leadership: A Sharing of Yourself.* Pittsburgh, Pa.: GTA Press, 1992.

Hackman, J. Richard, ed. *Groups That Work (and Those That Don't): Creating Conditions for Effective Teamwork.* San Francisco: Jossey-Bass, 1990.

Heider, J. *The Tao of Leadership: Leadership Strategies for a New Age.* New York: Bantam Books, 1986.

Kanter, Rosabeth Moss. "The New Managerial Work." *Harvard Business Review* 67, no. 6 (November/December 1989): 85–92.

Lacoursiere, R. B. *The Life Cycle of Groups.* New York: Human Science Press, 1980.

Lewin, K. "Group Decisions and Social Change." In *Readings in Social Psychology,* edited by Eleanor E. Maccoby et al., 197–211. New York: Holt, Rinehart, 1958.

Lieberman, M., et al. *Encounter Groups: First Facts.* New York: Basic Books, 1973.

Luft, J. *Group Process: An Introduction to Group Dynamics*. 2d ed. Palo Alto, Calif.: National Press Books, 1970.

Maddux, Robert B. *Team Building: An Exercise in Leadership*. Los Altos, Calif.: Crisp Publications, 1988.

Manz, Charles C. *Superleadership: Leading Others to Lead Themselves*. New York: Prentice Hall Press, 1989.

Marchington, Mick. *Successful Team Management: A Guide to Total Employee Involvement*. Cambridge, Mass.: Blackwell, 1992.

Margerison, Charles J. *Team Management: Practical New Approaches*. London: Mercury, 1990.

Mink, Oscar G., et al. *Groups at Work*. Englewood Cliffs, N.J.: Educational Technology Publications, 1987.

Quick, Thomas L. *Successful Team Building*. New York: AMACOM, 1992.

Rosen, Ned A. *Teamwork and the Bottom Line: Groups Make a Difference*. Hillsdale, N.J.: Lawrence Erlbaum Associates, 1989.

Schein, E. *Process Consultation*. Vols. 1 and 2. Reading, Mass.: Addison-Wesley, 1988.

Sundel, M., et al. *Individual Change Through Small Groups*. New York: New American Library, 1985.

Swap, Walter C., and Associates, ed. *Group Decision Making*. Beverly Hills, Calif.: Sage Publications, 1984.

Teeter, Deborah J., and G. Gregory Lozier, eds. *Pursuit of Quality in Higher Education: Case Studies in Total Quality Management*. San Francisco: Jossey-Bass, 1983.

Tjosvold, Dean. *Teamwork for Customers: Building Organizations That Take Pride in Serving*. San Francisco: Jossey-Bass, 1993.

Torres, Cresencio. *Self-Directed Work Teams: A Primer*. San Diego, Calif.: Pfeiffer, 1991.

Varney, Glenn H. *Building Productive Teams: An Action Guide and Resource Book*. San Francisco: Jossey-Bass, 1989.

Webb, Gisela M. "Implementing Team Management at the Texas Tech University Libraries." *Library Personnel News* 1, no. 4 (fall 1987): 39–40.

Wellins, Richard S. *Empowered Teams: Creating Self-Directed Work Groups That Improve Quality, Productivity, and Participation*. San Francisco: Jossey-Bass, 1991.

Notes

1. D. Carew et al., *The One Minute Manager Builds High Performing Teams* (San Diego, Calif.: Blanchard Training and Development, 1990), 39.

2. Ibid., 46.

3. Ibid., 57.

4. Ibid., 64.

5. Philip R. Harris, *Management in Transition* (San Francisco: Jossey-Bass, 1985), 240.

6. Carl E. Larson and Frank M. J. LaFasto, *Team Work: What Must Go Right / What Can Go Wrong* (Newbury Park, Calif.: Sage, 1989), 27.

7. R. T. Moran and Philip R. Harris, *Managing Cultural Synergy* (Houston, Tex.: Gulf, 1982), 128.

•••••••Chapter 6

Roles in the Team Management Library

"Let us endeavor so to live
that when we come to die
even the undertaker will be sorry."
—Samuel Langhorne Clemens (1835–1910)

Team Management in Libraries

A hierarchy stresses control, and team management stresses facilitation. Under team management, responsibility for the performance of work groups falls to the group rather than to the administration, as in a traditional hierarchy. Team members are involved in problem solving and do not rely solely on decisions from the administration. Another major difference between strict hierarchical structures and the collegial team approach to management is that team members must communicate with their peers within and outside the organization rather than relying on management as the sole source of information. Katherine W. Hawkins, in an article in *Library Administration & Management,* describes how a library can implement team management, emphasizing that both workers and management must be committed in order for the change to succeed.[1]

All academic libraries have a complement of librarians as well as professional, clerical, and student staffing. These groups are sometimes identified by different names, but regardless of the designations, one will find a mixture of positions in each department.

How do the different levels of staff deal with the team management environment? How is working in this environment different from working in the traditional hierarchy? How does team management shape the roles of authorities like the dean? This chapter discusses the various roles of staff and supervisors under team management and how each group thrives or fails in this environment.

81

Staffing

Academic libraries are more complex than many people realize. Not only are they complex in the range of services offered and technical functions performed, but their staffs are composed of a mix of librarians, specialists, technicians, and hourly workers, both regular and temporary. This mix of staff can be both a strength and a problem for library administrators. In a hierarchy, it is clear where each group belongs. In the team management environment, it is essential that all groups work closely together to accomplish departmental and library objectives and goals.

The student employees and hourly employees are clearly on the bottom rung in the hierarchy. In the team management environment, they are treated equal to all team members whose contributions are encouraged and highly valued. Technicians and specialists are typically exempt employees who perform tasks up to and including some, if not all, professional duties performed also by librarians. Often, they have gained expertise in their particular job responsibilities through years of experience. The librarians typically are the specialists in cataloging, acquisitions, reference, and administration and provide leadership for the library. The librarians are expected to have the same or more expertise than staff because they hold master's degrees in library science.

In a hierarchy, students and hourly staff report to exempt staff and librarians, exempt staff report to other exempt staff and librarians, and librarians in nonadministrative positions report to department heads and other administrators. In a flat organization or team management environment, all levels of staffing are closer to the top of the organization. Lines between the groups grow fuzzy, and therein lie potential problems. Some of the problems or conflicts are represented by artificial or arbitrary distinctions between librarians and staff. These conflicts are discussed in detail in chapter 7.

Library Faculty

A distinction must be drawn between the inexperienced librarian and the seasoned librarian who come into a team management environment, and between those librarians who come into a team management environment and those who are already working in a library that changes from a hierarchy to team management. A distinction will not be drawn between librarians who hold faculty status and those who do not, except to say that the team management environment can permit more flexibility in allowing library faculty to meet their faculty requirements.

The inexperienced or new librarian joining a team management library will not likely have experienced a hierarchical library organization. This librarian will naturally assume that all libraries are so administered and can provide "innocent" insights into the organization that others will appreciate. The inexperienced librarian may also have criticisms of team management that seasoned librarians counter with "Yes, but at my last library . . . ."

Some new librarians will thrive in an environment that permits them to greatly determine their own priorities within the framework of the library's goals, allowing them to contribute to the whole. Some new librarians need considerable structure and perform best in a hierarchy. The recruitment and selection of the right librarians for the team management environment are critical to their success, just as it is important to select the right librarians for a hierarchical organization.

Newly hired seasoned librarians, those who have a wide range of academic library experience, will bring their previous experience to bear on the team management environment. Again, whether they need structure or not will determine how well they succeed. Noticeable differences for librarians between the traditional hierarchy and team management will be that, under the latter, they will find less structure, fewer guidelines, and more opportunities to shape library policy and determine their own activities.

Under team management, librarians also will find themselves part of or closer to the decision-making process, if only because they will probably report to a department head who is directly involved in the top management team rather than to a traditional department head who reports to an assistant or associate dean or director.

Librarians working in a hierarchy that changes to team management are more affected than new hires, because those being recruited have the option of declining a position in the team management environment. Those already in the organization who desire structure may no longer have it, and those who desire more flexibility or even ambiguity will thrive. After a change to team management, some librarians who object to the change nonetheless will choose to stick with it. Although administrators and team members may wish these "hierarchical holdouts" would go away, if handled appropriately they may provide useful feedback to the new and various teams. Every organization needs individuals who can offer constructive criticism, becoming the conscience of the library. Conversely, the librarian who tries to undermine the organization must be dealt with appropriately. A discussion of resistance to change is provided in chapter 5.

The librarian in the Humanistic Management by Teamwork setting must be self-motivated and able to deal with less structure, or very little structure and direction. The concept of self-management is extremely important for librarians. Chapter 7 provides a further discussion of library faculty in the team management environment.

Professional Staff

For purposes of this discussion, professional staff are the highest-level staff that are usually engaged in reference, cataloging, and management activities. Generally, the highest-level staff are long-time employees of the library who have worked their way up through the ranks and may or may not have advanced degrees. Professional staff are critical to the successful implementation of team management. Their roles in the organization become pivotal in the everyday operation of the library. Because team management requires that the department heads and librarians are more heavily involved in library-wide team activities, professional staff must be able to manage many of the day-to-day operations. Many of these staff may be advanced to assistant department head positions, or they may manage those units that do not always require librarians as heads, such as circulation, interlibrary loan, or bindery positions.

Do professional staff have to buy into team management? Their importance to the success of team management cannot be overstated. More than just buying into team management, professional staff serve as role models to the technical staff and student employees. Along with librarians, professional staff set the agenda for the rest of the staff. The professional staff may resist the implementation of team management as strongly as or more strongly than librarians, yet staff probably have fewer alternatives than librarians (or library faculty) if they do not agree with the philosophy of team management. It is therefore extremely important to consult closely with professional staff, taking care to listen to their concerns. It is also important to recruit and select the right persons for advancement to supervisory positions.

The professional staff are also a critical resource in the successful systemwide management of the library. It is important that they be involved as much as possible in the decision-making processes of the library. This can be accomplished by including them as committee members on all but the faculty-specific committees such as those regarding tenure and promotion. Their contributions and cooperation are essential to spreading team management to all levels of the organization.

Technical Staff

Technical and clerical staff are normally the lower-level staff in the academic library, and turnover in those positions is second only to the positions held by student employees. Often, many of the technical and clerical staff are part-time and unionized. Depending on union requirements, employees holding technical and clerical positions may be effectively prohibited from functioning in non-unionized teams.

In some cases, technical and clerical staff are former student employees hired for part-time positions. Other staff are longtime employees, including some who may resist team management because they prefer more structure, and others who are quite accepting because they are in positions that receive direct supervision. They may, in fact, not be particularly affected by the management style, except that they are asked to participate in team meetings and team objectives. Technical and clerical staff are important to the departmental team. Many of the technical staff advance through the ranks to become tomorrow's professional staff members. They must be encouraged to contribute their ideas and support to the team.

Student Employees

Student employees differ from permanent staff in their work schedules, job duties, benefits, funding sources, and their planned impermanence. Their work schedules, usually 20 hours a week or less, must be arranged around classes that change each semester. Job duties are typically of the lowest level in the library. They are the most distant from the center of decision making and have the least commitment to the library. They are, after all, students who will earn degrees in their chosen fields, leaving the library with, we hope, lasting friendships and worthwhile work experiences.

Student employees are a critical part of the library's staffing and its ability to provide service. How do student workers fit into the team management environment? Student workers should be included in departmental staff meetings whenever possible and invited and encouraged to offer their opinions and suggestions on all matters affecting the department and their work. The communication media for the library should be shared with all student employees to keep them abreast of library news. Not surprisingly, student employees can provide insightful suggestions on departmental procedures and policies.

The Dean's Role

The dean or director is easily the most important person in the team management environment, without whom the team would not exist. The dean provides leadership for the top library management team. The dean normally chairs the meetings, although that task can be delegated or even rotated among the members. The dean must serve as the final arbiter in the event of lack of consensus; however, if the top library management team looks to the dean for all decisions, the team has failed to perform. Lack of consensus should be rare if the team is succeeding.

Regardless of how persons in the library view the role of the dean, all those outside the library view the dean as they do all other college deans—as the "responsible party." All matters relating to library administration and management are effectively the dean's responsibility, and it is the dean or library director that must represent the library's top management team and all of the library to the university administration, the faculty at large, and the public.

The implementation and practice of humanistic management by teamwork has to be initiated by the dean. The dean shares authority with the library's top management team, with department heads, and with staff at the dean's discretion. If the team fails, if the library staff fails, the dean is accountable and answerable. The library dean's role is extremely risky and not without pitfalls, but it is also not without rewards for all library employees.

By sharing the authority vested in that position, the dean must be able to depend on the library's management team, departmental teams, committees, and individuals to carry out the lion's share of daily operations and services. A team management environment requires that the dean not be a hands-on, must-know-everything, I-run-the-library type of person. Just as the dean shares authority, the management teams and individuals must assume responsibility and know where their authority begins and ends. Only through experience does it become evident where the lines of authority are drawn.

Department heads must be able to determine when an issue needs the top management team's advice or the dean's attention or both. Although we do not suggest that the dean be isolated from daily operations and decisions, it is incumbent upon the team members to know when the dean must be informed or consulted, or when an issue or problem can only be dealt with by the dean. The dean therefore must have tremendous trust in those who make those determinations. Nothing can be more problematic than for a vice president to call the dean on the carpet for something the dean should have known about but did not. No matter how much authority a department head assumes, the dean is ultimately responsible. Team members must be extremely sensitive to how the university administration views what the library does, and they must remember that, to the administration, the dean is "the" library administration.

The role of the dean in the team management environment is to monitor the top management team's progress and to guide it. The role of the dean outside the team management environment is the same as that of all library deans—to provide an interface between the library and the university and public. A team functioning at an optimal level can afford the dean the time to devote to that primary responsibility. In a hierarchy, assistant or associate deans have responsibility for daily operations. In the team management environment, the library's top management team shoulders that responsibility.

The Associate Dean's Role

Most academic library deans attained their positions because of their abilities to manage large groups of librarians, staff, and programs. The associate or assistant deans gain their experience in much the same manner as department heads or assistant directors. It is natural then to assume that the associate dean is accustomed to exercising authority and managing people. In a hierarchical organization, several associate deans have responsibility for the departments in technical services, public services, and collection development, for instance.

In the team management environment, the associate dean (if and when the library has one) must assume an unaccustomed role—serving in a staff rather than a line position. The traditional associate dean role as supervisor of department heads distances the department heads from the dean. In order for the top management team to be effective, members should report to the dean rather than the associate dean. In the team management environment, it is also more effective to have as few assistant deans as possible. We recommend that only one associate dean replace the traditional hierarchical assistant or associate deans, thereby eliminating the divisions that they traditionally oversee (e.g., collection, development, public sevices, and technical services).

The associate dean's role is similar to that of the dean in that the associate dean has many of the same responsibilities as the dean and acts in the dean's place in the absence of the dean. The associate dean has more responsibility than the dean for daily operations systemwide, yet most operational, personnel, and budgetary decisions are made at the departmental or team management group level. The associate dean's role under team management is largely that of facilitator, mediator, and adviser.

The dean and the associate dean are the point people for the library with regard to the administration and the public. By sharing authority and bestowing trust in the library's teams and individuals, the dean and associate dean can focus their efforts on programmatic and librarywide initiatives on behalf of the library. The authority exercised by these two officials is also discussed in chapter 4.

The Department Head's Role

In the team management environment, department heads will likely form the core of the library's top management team. In addition to department heads, the library management team will include directors of centers, branches, and major programs, as well as other key individuals such as automation, personnel, and budgetary office heads. For the purpose of this discussion, all members of the library's top management team are considered under the category of department head. A more complete discussion of the composition of the library management team is included in chapter 11.

The department head assumes new roles in the team management environment. In addition to all of the responsibilities of planning, organizing, staffing, and managing a department, this individual must assume responsibility for overall library management in partnership with the administration and the team. It requires the department head to think not only of the well-being of a given department but of the library as a whole. As a member of the library's manegement team and being a library-wide administrator, the department head is required to contribute and participate in library matters to a greater degree than the traditional department head. The development of an overall view of the library requires that jealousies and competition among and between departments be put aside. As members of the library's top management team gel as a unit, it is no longer necessary to compete for resources or attention. The team process encourages give and take among members, and, as trust develops, the department heads feel more secure in knowing that decisions are arrived at in a nonthreatening manner and are in the best interest of the library as a whole.

Under hierarchical management, staff are accustomed to seeing their department head charge like a knight in shining armor into the fray and come out with what the department needs—new equipment, staff, or funds. The staff expect their given department head to do battle with other department heads for the spoils of war. But as a member of the working library management team, the department head is required to envision the broader needs of the library. The department head must be able to return to staff and explain that another department needed a personal computer or a staff person more than they did. It is commonplace for the department head to succeed in the eyes of the library's management team and fail in the eyes of department staff, or vice versa. It is incumbent on the department head to educate staff in team management philosophy to help them understand the tightrope walk that is the department head's role. The department head would do well to develop the staff into a team that works like the library's top management team.

The success of team management in the library depends to a large degree on the performance of the department heads and their ability to handle the conflicting roles of library-wide team member and of being a specific department head. The department head cannot be overly protective of the department, nor can the department head give away the department farm. All members of the library-wide management team must contribute to the larger or greater good while furthering their respective departments' aims. The department head's position in team management is a challenging one, but it can be very rewarding.

Staff Department Heads

In the flat organizational structure of the team management environment, department heads report to the dean. Concerted efforts are made to involve team members in the everyday operational decisions of the various specific departments and of the library as a whole. In most instances, department heads are senior (faculty) librarians. In some cases, a librarian will head a department comprised exclusively of specialists, technicians, and student workers. What happens when that librarian is on sabbatical or other extended leave, or resigns? Often, the most qualified individual to take over the helm is a senior staff member. The result is that a senior staff member occupies a position higher than that of (for example) reference librarians and catalog librarians who report to other librarians. Does the staff member serving as acting department head have equal status with other department heads or a higher status than some faculty librarians? Will the university administration or the teaching faculty believe this is proper? In such situation, why should those librarians have faculty status anyway? The distinctions that must be drawn between staff and library faculty are detailed in chapter 7.

Staff Members' Roles

The staff members' roles in the team management environment depend in large part on their positions in the organization and on whether their departments utilize teams. The higher the level of the position, the more likely that a staff member will be involved in the library-wide management team. Because of the management and supervisory responsibilities of higher-level staff members, they will be keenly aware of the team management environment and will likely be team leaders themselves. Lower-level staff may be team members but are not as likely to be affected by team management. Staff are involved as team members and are expected to contribute as such. This includes working within the library's top management team to establish priorities and to discuss matters of concern regarding specific departments and the library in its broadest sense.

The department head is expected to conduct regular staff meetings to discuss issues being considered by the top library management team and to get feedback and relay staff concerns to the team. Staff members then are expected to participate in discussions, not only of concern regarding their respective departments, but also participate in discussions regarding library-wide matters. In the team management environment, staff must be involved.

In the team management environment, staff also are involved in library-wide task forces and committees, such as automation planning, collection development, technical services planning groups, and other planning and development activities. Talented staff can be identified and rewarded more easily in the team management environment because of the opportunities afforded by working with a larger number of staff and librarians on librarywide committees. The staff in the team management environment are closer to the circle of decision making than in the traditional hierarchy because of the absence of associate/assistant deans or directors in line positions. This also contributes to closer working relationships among the staff of former divisions (collection development, public services, and technical services), which are eliminated as distinct entities.

The staff are important to the success of team management in academic libraries. When team management is instituted, staff may not be affected as immediately as other library employee groups, but the differences in the organization will soon be noticed by even the lowest-level staff. After a period of adjustment, many of the staff will thrive in the flat organizational structure. Those who do hang onto their old ways generally will not adversely affect the overall success of team management in the library.

Team Management Is Not for Every Library

It would be presumptuous to suggest that library personnel in the team management environment are significantly different from library staff in a hierarchical library organization, but there are some differences, as pointed out in this chapter. The team management environment is not the best environment for those people who require a lot of structure, who resist change, who are unwilling to look beyond their own jobs, or who cannot work comfortably with others. It is also an inappropriate environment for supervisors who wish to exert authority and control over others or who are strict disciplinarians. The team management environment is not for everyone but can be very rewarding for many.

Bibliography

American Management Association. *Building a Winning Team: High Performance Through Teamwork.* New York: American Management Association, 1993.

Cargill, Jennifer, and Gisela M. Webb. *Managing Libraries in Transition.* Phoenix, Ariz.: Oryx Press, 1987.

Drucker, Peter F. "Effective Structures for the Management of Human Resources." *Australian Academic and Research Libraries* 16 (June 1985): 88–96.

Durrey, Peter. *Staff Management in University and College Libraries.* Oxford, England: Pergamon Press, 1976.

Evans, G. Edward. *Management Techniques for Librarians*. 2d ed. New York: Academic Press, 1983.

Howard, Helen. "Organization Theory and Its Applications to Research in Librarianship." *Library Trends* 32, no. 4 (spring 1984): 477–93.

Klingner, Donald E. "When the Traditional Job Description Is Not Enough." *Personnel Journal* 58 (April 1979): 243–48.

Lawrence, Paul R., and Jay W. Lorsch. *Organization and Environment: Managing Differentiation and Integration*. Rev. ed. Boston: Harvard Business School Press, 1986.

Lewis, David. W. "An Organizational Paradigm for Effective Academic Libraries." *College & Research Libraries* 47, no. 4 (July 1986): 337–53.

Martell, Charles R. *The Client-Centered Academic Library: An Organizational Model*. Westport, Conn.: Greenwood, 1983.

Martin, Lowell A. *Organizational Structure of Libraries*. Library Administration Series, 5. Metuchen, N.J.: Scarecrow Press, 1984.

McCabe, Gerard B. "Contemporary Trends in Academic Library Administration and Organization." In *Issues in Academic Librarianship: Views and Case Studies for the 1980's and 1990's*, edited by Peter Spyers-Duran and Thomas W. Mann, Jr., 21–35. Westport, Conn.: Greenwood, 1985.

Metcalf, Keyes D. "Departmental Organization in Libraries." In *Current Issues in Library Administration*, edited by Carlton B. Joeckel, 90–110. Chicago: University of Chicago, 1939.

Mussman, K. "Socio-technical Theory and Job Design in Libraries." *College & Research Libraries* 39, no. 1 (January 1978): 20–28.

Ricking, Myrl, and Robert E. Booth. *Personnel Utilization in Libraries: A Systems Approach*. Chicago: American Library Association, 1974.

Tunley, Malcolm. *Library Structures and Staffing Systems*. London: Library Association, 1979.

Notes

1. Kathrine W. Hawkins, "Implementing Team Management in the Modern Library," *Library Administration & Management* 3, no. 1 (winter 1989): 196.

•••••••Chapter 7

Library Faculty in the
Team Management Environment

"It is useless for the sheep to pass
resolutions in favor of vegetarianism
while the wolf remains of a different opinion."
—William Ralph Inge (1860–1954)

Job Responsibilities
of Librarians and Staff

In many libraries, the job responsibilities of librarians and staff overlap. Most noticeable are the responsibilities of librarians and non-librarians engaged in cataloging and reference. Friction between librarians and staff (non-librarians) results when, from all appearances, they are doing the same work for less than comparable compensation.

Catalogers, whether librarians or staff, often perform the same or similar range of cataloging activities—from Cataloging-in-Publication to original cataloging. Cataloging staff typically begin by learning how to handle Cataloging in Publication and Library of Congress records. Those who show the aptitude can be taught to work with consortia copy records. Some advance to learning how to do original cataloging with and then without revision by librarians per se. This level of cataloging is normally reserved for cataloging librarians, but who is to say that exempt staff cannot do original cataloging without the master's-level library course work required for librarians? Typically, librarians who are hired as catalogers should be expected to begin original cataloging within a relatively short time. Is the difference that staff attain sophisticated expertise through experience and librarians through education? After a period of six years, for example, should the two catalogers, staff and librarian, not be earning equal salaries? In some instances, should the staff member not be earning more, based on performance?

93

Reference librarians are hired and, after a brief period of becoming familiar with the physical layout and holdings of the department, are often scheduled for desk duty with a colleague and then alone. Exempt staff members are hired and, after a longer period of orientation and training, are scheduled for desk duty with a colleague and then alone. Reference librarians are hired for specialized scientific, business, fine arts, education, and humanities libraries with second master's degrees or specialized experience. Exempt staff are hired for those same libraries with subject master's degrees in those fields. However, they lack the library degree. After six years, for example, should the two persons in the reference department, staff and librarian, not be earning equal salaries? In some instances, should the staff member not be earning more, based on performance? Is it any wonder there is dissatisfaction among the staff who believe that they are being arbitrarily denied comparable pay for comparable work?

The differences between librarians and staff (non-librarians) may lie in their secondary duties. Librarians may have collection development, bibliographic instruction, and committee responsibilities. But do exempt staff not have the same capabilities as traditional librarians, given proper training and experience? In some libraries, certain staff members do perform those additional duties. Should staff members not be equally compensated? The difference appears to be that librarians can be expected to perform professional responsibilities based on their education, and staff members are only able to do so after years of on-the-job experience.

Conflict of Librarianship with Faculty Status

The differences between high-level staff and librarians with faculty status appear to be greater than between high-level staff and librarians who do not have faculty responsibilities (e.g., teaching, scholarship, and research). Faculty librarians have additional faculty requirements that must be met. The exempt, or professional, staff member is required to work the standard 35- to 40-hour workweek. Deviations from the standard workweek must be accounted for through approved leave (annual, sick, leave without pay, etc.). Faculty librarians are theoretically on a schedule similar to that of teaching faculty. In spite of the fact that faculty librarians are required to meet publication and service requirements, most are obligated to also adhere to the same workweek or workload as staff. Their absences for university committee meetings, conference attendance, and conducting research for publication are duly noted by staff members, and in some instances, are a source of major irritation. On the one hand, not only are the faculty librarians earning higher salaries for performing essentially the same work as staff, but also they do not appear, in the eyes of some staff, to be held to the standard workweek. On the other hand, staff members go home at the end of the day without care of scholarship or research requirements, while faculty librarians leave each day with worries of publications to be done and faculty requirements to be met. Librarians with faculty status face the conflict between pulling their share of departmental work and meeting tenure and promotion requirements. Sometimes the relationships between staff and librarians become understandably strained.

Collegial and Hierarchical Evaluation

In the team management environment, faculty librarians are required to meet stringent faculty requirements and submit to a tenure and promotion process equivalent to that of the teaching faculty, just as they would under a hierarchical system. That process typically involves a hierarchical evaluation by department chairs and deans as well as evaluation by peers or tenured faculty or both. How does the library's department head equate to the teaching department's chair? The dean in the nondepartmentalized college must be equivalent to the dean of the departmentalized college (for example, Arts and Sciences College with English, history, physics, etc., departments). Must the library dean write the evaluations of all library faculty? The peer review process is essential in the team management environment, but should staff input on library faculty evaluations be weighed equally with input from other library faculty? Should staff (non-librarians) be considered equals to librarians holding professorial rank in the team management environment but not when it comes to staff say regarding promotion and tenure evaluations of library faculty? Will the university administration or the teaching faculty think that staff evaluations of library faculty are proper? Why should those librarians have faculty status anyway? How are the professional staff and faculty librarians different? These questions concerning evaluation in the team management environment are thoroughly discussed in chapter 10.

Library Faculty vs. Library Staff

The expectations, requirements, and policies regarding library faculty members and library staff at the University of New Mexico General Library are enumerated in the following two lists. Taken together, the lists reveal (generally) the differences between the resonsibilities placed on library faculty and non-librarian staff in academic libraries.

Library Faculty at the University of New Mexico General Library

1. Library faculty members are recruited via national searches.

2. Library faculty members must have a master's degree in library science from an accredited American Library Association program.

3. Library faculty members are normally required to have prior experience at other academic or research libraries or both.

4. Library faculty members are expected to have a broad understanding of national library issues affecting libraries in the past, present, and future.

5. Library faculty members are guided by the *University of New Mexico Faculty Handbook*.

6. Library faculty members are required to serve a six-year probationary period before becoming a permanent employee.

7. Library faculty members are required to undergo peer evaluation for probationary, tenure, and promotional reviews.

8. Library faculty members are required to undergo peer evaluation by professional colleagues at other institutions.

9. Library faculty members, in order to be in compliance with the *University of New Mexico Faculty Handbook*, are required to publish and perform research activities.

10. Library faculty members are required to have a commitment to the library profession as demonstrated by professional activity. Library faculty members are expected to participate in professional organizations at the state, regional, or national levels, or all three.

11. Library faculty members are required to provide programmatic leadership in the library by participating in planning activities.

12. Departments are normally managed by library faculty members.

13. Library faculty members may be required to manage programs.

14. The library faculty have an understanding with the dean of library services that they have formed a partnership for the purpose of both sharing and discharging the responsibilities of the general library to its various constituencies. The faculty of the general library have the right of review and action in regard to the following:

    a. Formulation of goals and objectives

    b. Creation of new departments and divisions

    c. Major administrative changes and other matters that in the opinion of the dean of the library or the dean's delegate affect the library as a whole

    d. Policies of appointment, retention, tenure, dismissal, and promotion in academic rank

    e. Research policies

    f. General faculty welfare

    g. Selection and appointment of all library faculty

15. Library faculty members are expected to take an active role in library faculty governance by doing the following:

    a. Participating in monthly faculty meetings

    b. Participating in the development of library policy

    c. Contributing to library faculty committee work

    d. Participating on the library's faculty search committees

    e. Participating in the hiring of new faculty by providing written evaluations of candidates for faculty positions

    f. Participating in the peer evaluation process for probationary, tenure, and promotional reviews

    g. Participating in the annual tenured faculty review of untenured faculty

    h. Participating in the leadership of the library faculty by being willing to serve as presiding officer or secretary

16. Library faculty members may take an active role in university faculty governance.

17. Library faculty members may hold universitywide faculty senate office.

Library Staff at the University of New Mexico General Library

1. Staff are recruited locally.

2. Staff may have any undergraduate or graduate degree to meet the position requirements and may have a master's in library science degree from an accredited American Library Association program.

3. Staff are required to serve a six-month probationary period before becoming a permanant employee.

4. Staff are evaluated by their supervisors.

5. Staff are guided by the university's personnel policies.

6. Staff are expected to contribute to a wide variety of library committees.

7. Staff may participate in professional organizations at the state, regional, and national levels.

8. Staff may be required to manage programs and departments of the library.

9. Staff may participate in the development of library policy.

10. Staff may be elected or appointed to the library's staff governance group.

11. Staff may take an active role in university staff activities.

12. Staff may hold universitywide staff office.

Now that we have dutifully listed how faculty and staff positions are different, it should be reemphasized that in the team management environment, all faculty and staff are to be treated by the administration and each other with dignity and respect. There are different ranks among team members, but those ranks should not be uppermost in people's minds. Team members must be able to work together without regard to rank, position, or classification. Library faculty who feel they are better than staff members on the team will not succeed in the team management library.

One approach to recognizing staff contributions to the team management environment is to establish a representative staff organization. This group is designed to be advisory to the library's top management team and to provide an outlet for staff concerns. The bylaws of the staff organization at the University of New Mexico General Library are provided in chapter 8.

Faculty Organization

An important aspect of an organization composed of teams is self-governance. The library faculty at the University of New Mexico have adopted the following document:

University of New Mexico
General Library Faculty Organization Document

Preamble: The Library Faculty Organization Document represents an understanding between the Dean of Library Services and the Library Faculty that they have formed a partnership for the purpose of both sharing and discharging the responsibilities of the General Library to its various constituencies. The Document describes the way in which business will be conducted and reinforces the desire of the dean and the Faculty to work together to accomplish the goals and to support the mission of the General Library.

The mission of the University of New Mexico General Library is to provide library services which support the programs of the University for the benefit of the University community and the residents of New Mexico.

Faculty Organization: The faculty of the General Library have the powers assigned to it by the following document, and will have the right of review and action in regard to the following:

1. Formation of goals and objectives;

2. Creation of new departments and divisions;

3. Major administrative changes and other matters which in the opinion of the dean of the library or his/her delegate affect the Library as a whole;

4. Policies of appointment, retention, tenure, dismissal, and promotion in academic rank that coincide with the policies outlined in the *Faculty Handbook of the University of New Mexico* and in Section II of the "ACRL Model Statement of Criteria and Procedures or Appointment, Promotion in Academic Rank, and Tenure for College and University Librarians";

5. Research policies;

6. General faculty welfare;

7. The selection and appointment of all library faculty.

However, actions taken by the Library Faculty will be subject to the authority of the Regents in matters involving finance, personnel, and general university policy.

Section 1. Membership

(a) The General Library Faculty will consist of Librarians with the rank of Professor, Associate Professor, Assistant Professor, Lecturer and Instructor including part-time and temporary appointees, with a Master's degree or higher in a library science program accredited by the American Library Association. Any exception to this provision must be brought to the Library Faculty and approved by a two-thirds (2/3) majority of the voting faculty.

(b) No person holding an interim or temporary appointment will be a member of the voting faculty. Any exception to this provision must be brought to the Library Faculty and approved by a two-thirds (2/3) majority of the voting faculty.

(c) The official list of the Library Faculty members, as defined above, designating both tenured and voting members, will be prepared by the Library Personnel Specialist at the request of the Secretary of the Library Faculty at the beginning of each academic year and will be updated when new faculty are appointed and when terminations take effect.

Section 2. Officers

(a) The presiding officer of the Library Faculty will be elected at the first faculty meeting of the academic year by a majority of the voting faculty and will serve for one year.

(b) In the absence of the presiding officer, the Library Faculty will elect an interim chair.

(c) The secretary of the Library Faculty will be elected by a majority of the voting members present at the March faculty meeting and will serve for one year beginning in July. The Secretary will be responsible for requesting the official list of faculty members, keeping and distributing copies of the minutes of each meeting, and distributing agenda for meetings of the Library Faculty at least two (2) working days before each meeting. The Faculty Secretary will submit an annual report to the faculty and will submit for inclusion in the General Library Official Bulletin all standing committee annual reports, the Secretary's annual report, and standing committee assignments.

Section 3. Meetings

(a) The Library Faculty will meet on a regular basis, as needed, but not less than once per quarter. A majority of the voting membership will constitute a quorum.

(b) Announcements of Library Faculty meetings will be made at least ten (10) working days in advance. Agenda items should be submitted to the Secretary at least five (5) working days before the meeting.

(c) An emergency meeting may be called by a written request of five (5) of the voting faculty and will be scheduled within five (5) working days.

(d) Special meetings may be called by the dean at any time.

Section 4. Committees

(a) The Library Faculty shall have Standing Committees. A list of Standing Committees is appended to the end of the Document.

(b) Committee on Committees: The Library Faculty will elect three (3) faculty members to serve on the Committee on Committees at the first faculty meeting of the academic year. They will serve for two years. The Secretary of the Library Faculty, the Presiding Officer, and the dean or designate will be ex officio members. The Committee on Committees is responsible for making appointments to Standing Committees, for recommending appointments to Search Committees, and for presenting faculty issues to the Library Faculty.

(c) Search Committees: In consultation with the Library Management Team and the Committee on Committees, the dean will be responsible for appointing the Chair and membership of search committees. Formation and composition of all search committees will be announced in the General Library Official Bulletin by the Faculty Secretary.

(d) All other committees will be chaired and members appointed by the appropriate individual(s) and announced in the General Library Official Bulletin by the committee chair.

Section 5. General

This document may be amended by a two-thirds (2/3) vote of the voting faculty. Proposal for amendments will be announced in advance of the meeting at which they will be discussed and tabled for thirty (30) days before final action.

The Presiding Officer shall be responsible for the Library Faculty's adherence to this document.

Faculty Committees

Curriculum Committee

Composition: Five faculty members of which at least three are tenured. Appointed by the Committee on Committees.

Purpose: To review all new course proposals for the purpose of ensuring that all courses fit within the instructional goals of the library and to assist course developers.

Faculty Professional Enrichment Committee

Composition: Seven faculty members appointed by the Committee on Committees.

Purpose: Develop procedures for and distribute travel funds to faculty.

Library Instruction Committee

Composition: Faculty and staff members representing public services areas engaged in library instruction.

Purpose: To provide training for library instructors, share resources, improve and coordinate library instruction.

Research and Publications Committee

Composition: A minimum of six members, one of whom is a staff member. Appointed by the Committee on Committees and the Library Professional Staff Advisory Council.

Purpose: To encourage and facilitate research and publication among library faculty, especially new faculty. Serve as a clearinghouse for information, sponsor workshops and seminars on research methodology and on research in progress.

Sabbatical Review Committee

Composition: Five to seven library faculty members, the majority of whom shall be tenured. The chair shall be tenured.

Purpose: To review requests for sabbaticals and make recommendations to the dean.

Tenure and Promotion Committee

Composition: Seven elected library faculty members: five tenured and two nontenured.

Purpose: Conduct promotion, code three, tenure, and post-tenure reviews of library faculty. Make recommendations to the dean.

Conditions of Employment

It may be necessary to clarify in no uncertain terms what is expected of all library faculty in the team management environment. Although the dean is viewed as the chief administative authority in the library by university administration, peer reviews and shared authority under team management may cause difficulties with tenure and promotion matters. The conditions of employment agreement can head off complaints at probationary and tenure reviews, such as "No one told me what was expected." Professor Robert L. Migneault, dean of library services at UNMGL, proposed the following document spelling out assumptions, beliefs, expectations, and requirements relating to conditions of employment.

Proposed Document for
Conditions of Employment

Assumptions

Whoever accepts a faculty appointment is qualified, willing, and able to carry out in good faith the responsibilities and duties commensurate with the appointment.

Whoever accepts a library faculty appointment in the library is a professionally qualified, academic research-oriented librarian.

Whoever accepts any faculty appointment in the library is subject to the same and comparable conditions of employment as library faculty holding the master's degree in library science.

Beliefs

Once hired, each library faculty member is capable of being a responsible and competent professional library employee.

Each library faculty member can and should perform and behave with professional integrity, enthusiasm, and in good faith for the welfare of the library and, by extension, the university.

Each library faculty member knows and understands well enough what that member's responsibilities and duties are, as well as what is expected to satisfactorily meet all necessary job requirements of the university and the library. This includes requirements pertaining to retention, promotion, and tenure.

Each library faculty member knows, at least instinctively, what they should and should not do to retain their positions, gain salary increases, move up the academic and professional ranks, and secure permanent employment. If and when library faculty members are uncertain or troubled about their job responsibilities, duties, expectations, or related matters, all library faculty members are socialized enough, knowledgeable enough, and resourceful enough to ask the proper questions, respond appropriately to advice and direction received, and otherwise carry on successfully for the good of the library.

Expectations

I expect each library faculty member to be professional and to think and act independently. In this professional and independent context, a library faculty member is to perform and act on the job in the manner expected by the dean of library services and the dean's designees, even if the library faculty member has not received instructions directly or has not been provided with expectations delineated in writing.

If and when a library faculty member does not know something that they realize or feel that they should know, I expect the library faculty member to consider it their responsibility to find out and act appropriately.

Whatever the library faculty member does or does not do relative to their official job responsibilities, duties, and concomitant expectations determines their rewards or other consequences or both. I expect each library faculty member to understand and accept the reality that, unless officially specified otherwise, all behavior and activities in or related to the library are subject to the legal and official authority or sanction or both, of the dean of library services and the dean's designees.

Requirements

All library faculty members are subject to the legal and official requirements of the university or the library or both. As ignorance of the law is no excuse, so is it with organizational requirements.

Performance Evaluation

All library faculty members are subject to annual or other performance evaluations. The performance evaluations of library faculty members may be conducted by the dean of library services or the dean's designees or both. Each performance evaluation will cover a specified period of time and will not necessarily reflect or affect the outcome of previous or subsequent evaluations. Performance evaluations may be done by line supervisors or by one's peers and colleagues or by both.

All performance evaluations of and by library faculty are subject to consideration by the dean of library services and are not necessarily binding on the dean.

Salary Determination

Salaries for library faculty members are subject to the legal and official authority and sanction of the dean of library services. Salary increases are subject to university guidelines, merit considerations, and equity or market adjustments or both. Salary increases based on equity or market adjustments or both do not necessarily reflect merit.

Appointment, Retention, Promotion, Tenure, and Post-Tenure Status

All decisions pertaining to the aforementioned are subject to the legal and official authority and sanction of faculty or the dean of library services or both.

Library Faculty Appointment, Position, and Job

It is assumed that the acceptance of a library faculty appointment in the library is voluntary. This act of one's own volition and the implications thereof apply to resignation as well.

The job of each library faculty member is to fulfill the responsibilities, carry out the duties, and meet concomitant expectations officially assigned to and associated with the library faculty member's given position.

Faculty rights and privileges are effectively linked to one's faculty or academic appointment, not to the given position held, nor to the responsibilities and duties of one's given position per se. The authority and accountability relative to one's given position are subject to the legal and official authority and sanction of one's administrative superior or superiors—at the library, the dean of library services.

Officially and technically, each library faculty member is a member of and employee in the library, effectively a nondepartmentalized college. Positions and job responsibilities and duties of each library faculty member may be changed as deemed necessary within the context of the General Library system as a whole.

Summary

1. Library faculty conditions of employment are manifested by the expressions linked herein to assumptions, beliefs, expectations, and requirements.

2. Library faculty are appointed because they are professionally and academically qualified, willing, and able to carry out in good faith the responsibilities and duties commensurate with the library faculty appointment in the library.

3. Once hired, each library faculty member is capable of and must be a professionally responsible and competent professional library employee.

4. Each library faculty member is personally responsible for knowing and successfully meeting the criteria for retention, promotion, tenure, and post-tenure conditions of employment.

5. Each library faculty member is personally responsible for knowing and successfully meeting the legal and official requirements of the university and of the library.

6. Each library faculty member is personally responsible for knowing and abiding by library policies and procedures that pertain to their library faculty appointment, position, and job.

7. Each library faculty member is personally responsible and accountable for their own behavior and actions on and related to their library faculty appointment, position, and job. One's behavior and actions determine one's rewards (e.g., promotion

or salary increases or both) or other consequences (e.g., change of position, reassignment of responsibilities and duties, no salary increase, dismissal) or both.

8. Each library faculty member is subject to annual or performance evaluations or both. These evaluations may be conducted by line supervisors or by one's peers and colleagues or both. Performance evaluations are to cover specified periods of time and will not necessarily have any bearing on previous or subsequent evaluations or both. All performance evaluations are subject to consideration by the dean of library services; however, they are not necessarily binding on the dean.

I have read and agree to the conditions of employment contained herein.

Signature _____

Date _____

Setting Library Faculty Salaries

In order to hire and retain the best library faculty possible, the library administration should attempt to pay its faculty as well as possible. One method of determining faculty salaries is to make market adjustments. Salaries in the team management environment are based on a policy developed by the library faculty organization. Actual salaries are set in accordance with the policy by the top library management team in partnership with the dean. The dean of library services appoints a salary review board to review faculty and staff salaries annually and make recommendations on correcting inequities.

Components of Library Faculty Salaries

University policy, as well as state and federal law and regulations, forbid unlawful discrimination on the basis of race, color, religion, national origin, physical or mental abilities, age, sex, sexual preference, ancestry, or medical condition, in recruiting, hiring, training, promotion, and all other terms and conditions of employment. UNMGL policies are administered in accordance with the university's affirmative action policy.

University policy describes the components of library faculty salaries but does not prescribe how salaries are set. The annual base salary is that salary figure that appears on the faculty contract. Salaries for library faculty members may be composed of some or all of the following elements, not necessarily in order of importance:

- Starting salary. The library faculty member's starting salary is determined by market, by internal and external equity for like positions, and by negotiation.

- Market. A library faculty member's salary may be adjusted because of market. A position requiring specialized skills for which there is a nationwide shortage may receive a market increase, independent of all other elements. Market increases become part of the annual base salary.

- Across-the-board. That portion of the salary increase determined by across-the-board (cost of living) increases is normally at the direction of the university administration. An explanation must be provided to the individual and to Academic Affairs when the standard across-the-board increase is not given. Across-the-board increases become part of the annual base salary.

- Equity. Differences in salaries for the same positions are not necessarily inequitable. All library faculty members' salaries are reviewed and inequities examined. Equity adjustments become part of the annual base salary.

- Merit. The determination of merit focuses on performance. It is guided by the merit criteria document approved by the UNMGL faculty. Merit increases become part of the annual base salary.

- Promotion. Salary increases resulting from promotion to associate professor or professor become part of the annual base salary.

- Temporary salary adjustment. Temporary salary adjustments made for acting administrative positions do not become part of the annual base salary but are made for specific periods of time.

- Special compensation. Special payments made for specific activities, for example, the regents lectureship, are normally onetime payments and are never made a part of the annual base salary.

The dean of library services has the authority and responsibility to reassign library faculty members in the General Library as needed. Such reassignments may result in salary adjustments.

Procedure for Salary Increases

The following steps are taken in setting library faculty salaries:

- Prior to notification of salary funds available, the salary review board meets to review all faculty salaries to identify perceived inequities. The committee, appointed by the library dean, includes three library department heads and two nondepartment-head library faculty members.

- The committee presents the information to the top library management team for discussion, with recommendations to the dean.

- Merit recommendations for nondepartment-head library faculty members are made to the library management team by the respective department heads.

- Department head merit recommendations are developed by the dean and reviewed by a subcommittee of the library management team.

- All library faculty members' merit recommendations are based on the merit criteria document adopted by the General Library faculty.

Salary Appeal Process

The following procedure is observed when a salary amount is being appealed:

- A memorandum is sent to each library faculty member, explaining how salaries were determined and how the individual's salary was calculated.

- Questions about salaries are directed to the department head or to the director of administrative services.

- An appeal of a salary amount is directed first to the department head and, if not resolved at that level, to the dean of library services.

- If an individual wishes to seek outside assistance, for example, by contacting university administration, the library will respond by providing all of the assistance and information necessary for resolution. Questions of pay inequity are thoroughly investigated.

Library Faculty Merit Criteria

The library faculty at UNM have adopted the following document to be used in the establishment of merit for all faculty:

University of New Mexico General
Library Merit Criteria Guidelines for Faculty

The categories for merit recommendations are the same as those used for promotion and tenure:

1. Librarianship

2. Scholarship, research, and creative work

3. Service

Librarianship/Teaching

The faculty member should show evidence of performing above average in this area. Performing one's job at a minimal level is not considered meritorious.

Each faculty member must have a statement of job responsibilities which will be the starting point for evaluating that faculty member. During the evaluation period each year, the faculty member and supervisor will review the statement of job responsibilities and set objectives to be achieved in the coming year.

The statement of job responsibilities and the agreed-upon objectives will form the basis for determining how well the individual has performed in the area of librarianship. Some suggestions for the supervisor to consider in evaluating the fulfillment of objectives established for the previous year are listed below. Since job responsibilities differ, care should be taken to apply these criteria as they relate to the faculty member's job responsibilities and objectives:

- —Development and implementation of techniques or methods which result in significant improvements in services or operations in the library.

- —Ability to perform functions in a creative and innovative fashion and/or to introduce innovative procedures, techniques, etc.

- —Productivity combined with quality.

- —Contribution of job performance to the overall performance and enhancement of the unit.

- —Evaluation of the faculty member based on feedback from library patrons, colleagues, and library employees.

- —Honors and awards presented to the faculty member (awards are not included if only for travel, i.e., Professional Enrichment Awards).

- —Grants received for library materials, facilities, equipment, and supplies.

- —Job-related library committees.

If any of the activities listed below are stated as job objectives, they will be included under the category of librarianship/teaching.

- —In-house reports and guides.

- —Relevant activities which enhance knowledge of new developments in areas related to the person's job such as credit courses, seminars, workshops, short courses.

- —Teaching of UNM courses.

- —Consulting, for example, review and assessment of programs in other institutions; providing instruction or conferring with offcampus visitors about specific library operations or services within the individual's statement of job responsibilities.

Scholarship, Research, and Creative Work

The quantity of work in any one year is not the determining factor in the evaluation. The crucial factors are the quality of work and its research or creative value as demonstrated by publication, public display, or performance. Scholarship in library science or in subject specialties is to be considered. Scholarship, research, and creative work are of equal value. Work in progress is also to be considered. The statement of job responsibilities and the agreed-upon objectives will form the basis for determining how well the individual has performed in the area of scholarship, research, and creative work.

A suggested ranking follows:

- —Books authored or coauthored

- —Refereed journal articles authored or coauthored

- —Books edited

- —Invited essays or chapters

- —Chapters authored or coauthored

- —Refereed proceedings (full paper or abstracts)

- —Presentations of papers

- —Research grants

- —Awards and honors for research activities (awards are not included if only for travel, i.e., Professional Enrichment Awards)

- —Unrefereed journal articles authored or coauthored

- —Reviews of manuscripts for scholarly publications

- —Editing, compiling, and indexing of substantial published works

- —Working papers

- —Book reviews

- —Contributions to abstracts and indexes

- —Articles in newsletters

- —Letters to the editor

- —Works in progress (ranked according to the type of work, completion to date, and potential for publication)

Other areas which may be considered as part of the evaluation of research and other creative activities are:

- —Participation in scholarly activities of academic or professional organizations, such as conducting lectures, workshops, seminars, and poster sessions

- —Advanced degrees earned

- —Bibliographies or databases for publication or dissemination

- —Translations

Service

Service may include service to the university community, activity in professional organizations on an international, national, regional, state, or local level, and service to the civic community. The statement of job responsibilities and the agreed-upon objectives will form the basis for determining how well the individual has performed in the area of service.
Considerations in this area:

- —Quantity and quality of the individual's contribution to the functioning of the university or professional organization (weight should be given to the type of participation as officer, chairperson, committee member, etc.)

- —Credit should also be given for membership on committees or attendance at meetings

Weighting of the Criteria

The goal of the document is to establish a range of criteria which would allow for 0 merit raise to exceptional merit raise. Librarianship will be considered the most heavily weighted of the three areas. Individuals must achieve the minimum standard of excellence in librarianship before they may be considered for merit in any other area. Merely a standard performance in this area will result in a 0 merit raise. Scholarship and service should not offset inadequate job performance nor should the outstanding performer's job be jeopardized by failure to publish and/or perform service activities during any one year. However, it is expected that faculty will show progress over time in all three areas.

The following range of weights will be used:

Criteria	Weight
Librarianship	60%
Research	25%
Service	15%

Note: After this proposal has been in place for three years, it would be desirable each year to average the person's merit over a three-year period in order to avoid penalizing a faculty member who was exceptionally meritorious in a year in which the amount of money available for merit was very small.

Mentoring

The following document regarding mentoring in the team management environment was developed by the University of New Mexico General Library:

Faculty Sponsor Program

Recognizing the need to assist those faculty members who have been appointed to a tenure track position in the UNM General Library, a faculty sponsor program has been created. The sponsor program is designed to assist faculty members in their progress toward code three reviews.

No later than two months after the tenure track appointment, the Promotion and Tenure Committee, with input from the faculty member, will select a sponsor for the faculty member. The sponsor should not be the faculty member's supervisor and preferably not be in the same department.

A sponsor should be an individual who has successfully completed at least the code three review at the General Library. The sponsor's responsibilities include the following:

- Serve as a friendly counselor

- Advise, encourage, and assist the faculty member in adjusting to the new environment

- Make the necessary introductions and arrange for orientation

- Help guide professional development

- Help the faculty member prepare for faculty reviews

- Participate in the six-month advisement review of the newly appointed faculty member

A sponsor should help the newly appointed faculty member maintain a proper balance in fulfilling the library's requirements of faculty status. A sponsor should serve in this appointment until at least the code three review and may continue to the tenure review. The sponsor or the Promotion and Tenure Committee can specifically request to terminate the sponsor agreement.

Preserving the Team Management Environment

Faculty, staff, and student workers all have a responsibility to work as members of the team. Failure to fulfill responsibilities could result in the demise of Humanistic Management by Teamwork. It is comparatively easy to simply "coast" or bide one's time in a hierarchy, but simply existing without active commitment and active participation in the team management environment is virtually impossible.

Constant vigilance must be maintained in the team management environment to ensure that the staffing groups in the library are balanced. The library management team, the faculty organization, the professional staff organization, and the administration have a responsibility to see that the roles of faculty and staff are clearly defined while at the same time facilitating team operations.

The top library management team, in partnership with the administration, has to guard against the blurring of faculty and staff roles and responsibilities. The library faculty have an obligation to maintain their faculty status and to carefully conform to the faculty requirements of the university. The senior faculty have a responsibility to see that only qualified junior faculty are tenured and to participate fully in library faculty and university faculty governance. The staff and their representative body have a responsibility to fully communicate their concerns to the library management team and the administration and to actively promote change when needed. All concerned must work diligently at making Humanistic Management by Teamwork succeed.

Bibliography

Ackerman, Page. "Governance and Academic Libraries." *Library Research* 2, no. 1 (spring 1981): 3–28.

Anderson, A. J. *Problems in Library Management*. Littleton, Colo.: Libraries Unlimited, 1981.

Boaz, Martha, ed. *Current Concepts in Library Management*. Littleton, Colo.: Libraries Unlimited, 1979.

Brown, Nancy A. "Managing the Coexistence of Hierarchical and Collegial Governance Structures." *College & Research Libraries* 46, no. 6 (November 1985): 478–82.

Dougherty, Richard M. "Personnel Needs for Librarianship's Uncertain Future." In *Academic Libraries by the Year 2000: Essays Honoring Jerrold Orne*, edited by Herbert Poole, 107–18. New York: R. R. Bowker, 1977.

Dougherty, Richard M., et al. *Scientific Management of Library Operations*. 2d ed. Metuchen, N.J.: Scarecrow Press, 1982.

Galvin, Thomas J., and Beverly Lynch, eds. *Priorities for Academic Libraries*. San Francisco: Jossey-Bass, 1987.

Georgi, Charlotte, and Robert Bellanti, eds. *Excellence in Library Management*. New York: Haworth Press, 1985.

Gore, Daniel. "Things Your Boss Never Told You About Library Management." *Library Journal* 102 (April 1, 1977): 765–70.

Harvey, John F., and Peter Spyers-Duran. *Austerity Management in Academic Libraries*. Metuchen, N.J.: Scarecrow Press, 1984.

Holley, Edward G. "Defining the Academic Librarian." *College & Research Libraries* 46, no. 6 (November 1985): 462–68.

Hyatt, James A., and Aurora A. Santiago. *University Libraries in Transition*. Washington, D.C.: National Association of College and University Business Officers, 1987.

Jones, Ken. *Conflict and Change in Library Organizations: People, Power and Service*. London: Bingley, 1984.

Ladd, Dwight R. "Myths and Realities of University Governance." *College & Research Libraries* 36, no. 2 (March 1975): 97–105.

Line, Maurice B. *Academic Library Management*. London: Library Association, 1990.

Lomas, Tim. *Management Issues in Academic Libraries*. London: Rossendale, 1986.

Lyle, Guy R. *The Administration of the College Library*. 4th ed. New York: H. W. Wilson, 1974.

Lynch, Beverly P. "Libraries as Bureaucracies." *Library Trends* 27, no. 3 (winter 1979): 259–67.

MacCrimmon, Kenneth R., and Donald A. Ehrenburg. *Taking Risks: The Management of Uncertainty*. New York: Free Press, 1988.

McElroy, A. Rennie. *College Librarianship*. Phoenix, Ariz.: Oryx Press, 1984.

Moran, Barbara B. *Academic Libraries: The Changing Knowledge Centers of Colleges and Universities*. Washington, D.C.: Association for Study of Higher Education, 1984.

Munn, Robert F. "The Bottomless Pit, or the Academic Library as Viewed from the Administration Building." *College & Research Libraries* 29, no. 1 (January 1968): 51–54.

Rizzo, John R. *Management for Librarians: Fundamentals and Issues*. Westport, Conn.: Greenwood, 1980.

Rogers, Rutherford D., and David C. Weber. *University Library Administration*. New York: H. W. Wilson, 1971.

Shaughnessy, Thomas W. "Technology and the Structure of Libraries." *Libri* 32, no. 2 (June 1982): 144–55.

Stueart, Robert D., ed. *Academic Librarianship: Yesterday, Today, Tomorrow*. New York: Neal-Schuman, 1982.

Stueart, Robert D., and Barbara B. Moran. *Library Management*. 3d ed. Littleton, Colo.: Libraries Unlimited, 1987.

Thompson, James, and Reg Carr. *An Introduction to University Library Administration*. 4th ed. London: Bingley, 1987.

Veaner, Allen B. *Academic Librarianship in a Transformational Age: Program, Politics, and Personnel*. Boston: G. K. Hall, 1990.

Vosper, Robert. "Library Administration on the Threshold of Change." In *Issues in Library Administration*, edited by Warren M. Tsuneishi et al., 37–51. New York: Columbia University Press, 1974.

Wasserman, Paul, and Mary Lee Bundy, eds. *Reader in Library Administration*. Washington, D.C.: Microcard Editions, 1968.

Weisbord, Marvin R. *Productive Workplaces: Organizing and Managing for Dignity, Meaning, and Community*. San Francisco: Jossey-Bass, 1987.

Willard, D. D. "Seven Realities of Library Administration." *Library Journal* 101, no. 1 (January 15, 1976): 311–17.

Zaltman, Gerald, ed. *Management Principles for Nonprofit Agencies and Organizations*. New York: AMACOM, 1979.

•••••••• Chapter 8

Communication in the Team Management Environment

"A community is like a ship;
everyone ought to be prepared to take the helm."
—Henrik Ibsen (1828–1906)

Facilitation Through Communication

Team management stresses facilitation, whereas the hierarchy stresses control. In the team management environment, there is vertical communication, but a greater emphasis is placed on horizontal communication. Individuals in the team management environment are encouraged to communicate across departmental and faculty-staff lines in many ways. Participative decision making in teams encourages frequent interaction within and among teams, work groups, and interest groups. Communication is facilitated by the top library management team, the library faculty organization, the staff organization, departmental management teams, monthly reports, an internal newsletter, task groups, and committees.

The Library Management Team

The top library management team is the library's main administrative decision-making group and is, technically, advisory to the dean. The size and composition of the library management team allow the group to make decisions based on the best information available. This alleviates the problems typical of small, administrative decision-making groups, which often must return to their department heads for additional information or which simply make decisions without having the necessary information. The team virtually eliminates the "us versus them" problems between department heads and library administrators.

The top library management team also facilitates improved communication among department heads, branch and center directors, functional specialists, administrators, and the dean. The library management team, which meets weekly, is able to develop effective communication among members, a quality that is often not evident in libraries where department heads report to assistant deans or directors for collection development, public services, and technical services. The lines between divisions disappear when library management team members are involved in the library-wide administrative decision-making process. Horizontal communication among the library's managers and administration provides a mechanism for more informed, more efficient decision making and improves the likelihood that decisions will be supported by departmental staff.

The Library Faculty Organization

The library faculty organization has responsibility in the team management environment for addressing all faculty issues. All faculty members on the top library management team are also members of the library faculty organization. In the team management environment, it is very important that the library management team and the library faculty organization take care to separate those issues that relate to the faculty status of librarians and those that are library management issues.

The library faculty organization develops policies relating to faculty, and the library management team develops policies relating to library management. A third group, the library professional staff advisory council, deals specifically with issues relating to staff. The relationship between the library management team and the library professional staff advisory council is closer than the relationship between the library faculty organization and the advisory council for two reasons. First, the library professional staff advisory council is advisory to the library management team, and the library faculty organization is not. Second, the staff group normally deals with conditions of employment, and the faculty group concerns itself with broader faculty and professional issues. Communication among library faculty members is enhanced by the library faculty organization, where faculty department heads and faculty nondepartment heads participate. In this organization, the professorial rank of faculty members is more important than their position in the library. The library faculty organization is discussed in greater detail in chapter 7.

The Library Professional Staff Advisory Council

The library professional staff advisory council is a representative group that deals specifically with staff issues in the team management environment. This elected group initiates programs of interest to library staff. It may decide to focus on staff development issues. Or it may wish to develop and recommend policies and procedures of concern to library staff to the top library management team for consideration. Essentially, the council is advisory to the library management team and is occasionally asked by the team to address specific issues of interest to staff and to report back to the team. At UNM, the library management team asked the council to develop advanced-level library specialist job descriptions and to develop merit criteria for salary discussions. The council has sponsored numerous staff development programs for staff and faculty. The bylaws of the council in the document below were written and approved by the library staff at large.

Bylaws of the Library
Professional Staff Advisory Council

Article I: Name

The name of this organization shall be the Library Professional Staff Advisory Council.

Article II: Object

The object of the Library Professional Staff Advisory Council shall be to act in an advisory capacity to the dean and library management team; to promote and implement library goals; to foster and support greater professionalism among library staff; and to foster and encourage collegiality among all groups within the library.

Article III: Membership

The membership of the Library Professional Staff Advisory Council shall consist of seven members elected from the nonfaculty staff not covered by the bargaining unit, and ex officio members consisting of the dean, associate dean, and head of administrative services. Elected members shall serve for a term of two academic years and may be reelected.

Beginning in the Fall of 1988, elections for three members will be held annually. In the case of a tie vote, a runoff election shall be held. The head of administrative services will conduct the elections and notify elected members. During alternate years, an additional member will be appointed to the Council by the dean.

When a permanent vacancy occurs, a special election will be held to fill the vacancy. For temporary vacancies of one year or less, the member vacating the position shall appoint a replacement with the approval of the Council to complete the term.

Procedures for electing new members of the Council will be as follows:

1. A list of all exempt staff will be made available in the General Library Official Bulletin (GLOB). Anyone listed who is not interested in serving on the Council or participating in any other committee will let the administrative assistant in the dean's office know that they do not wish to be listed on any election ballot.

2. A second listing of all professional staff will be distributed which will be used as a ballot for electing new Council members.

3. Votes will be tabulated by the head of administrative services, and the Council will notify the new members, who will begin their terms with the Council at the next scheduled meeting.

Article IV: Officers

The Library Professional Staff Advisory Council shall have no formal officers; however, one member may be chosen to serve as chair as needed on an ad hoc basis.

Article V: Meetings

The meetings shall be held once a month or more frequently as needed. Regular monthly meetings shall be open. Minutes shall be taken by elected members on a rotating basis. Minutes shall be published in the General Library Official Bulletin.

Article VI: Committees

The Library Professional Staff Advisory Council shall nominate committee members for appointment by the dean to accomplish specific tasks and projects as needed.

Article VII: Amendment of Bylaws

These bylaws may be amended at any time by consensus of all elected members of the Library Professional Staff Advisory Council.

Departmental Management Teams

An important aspect of the team management environment is communication in departmental teams. All departments, centers, and branches are expected and required to conduct weekly departmental team meetings. The team leader, who is also a top library management team member, is responsible for discussing management issues with the departmental management team members. This takes the form of a report on what the top library management team decided at its last meeting and discussion of pending issues. The departmental team leader gathers needed information from departmental team members in order to contribute to the top management team discussion and decisions and to lead discussion on how the department will implement various decisions. Communication with departmental team members is direct, because the department head is actively involved in library-wide decision making rather than simply passing on what a traditional divisional associate dean has reported. All team members are close to the decision making in the team management environment. The newsletter, discussed later in this chapter, reinforces and in some cases clarifies decisions made by the top management team. Whether the library department, center, or branch is organized as a team, a hierarchy, or a combination of both, communication at the departmental level is improved in the team management environment because of the elimination of the traditional divisional associate/assistant dean or director levels in the organization.

Departmental Monthly Reports

All library departments, centers, and branches are required to produce monthly departmental reports that are routed to all other departments. The purpose of monthly reports is to communicate departmental activities to the rest of the library. The reports normally include a department head overview of the activities and accomplishments of the department, individual reports from departmental team members, and departmental statistics. These reports serve not only to inform others of departmental activity but also to provide the opportunity for individuals to share information with others. Monthly reports serve as the basis for the department's annual report.

The Internal Newsletter

The library-wide newsletter in the team management environment is a product of contributions from library faculty and staff, committees, and the top library management team. Typically, a library's newsletter is developed in the dean's office, and often the dean or director has control over its content. However, at UNM, the newsletter, titled the GLOB, for General Library Office Bulletin, is produced by the administrative assistant in Administrative Services. The newsletter includes brief announcements and news items contributed by individual library faculty and staff. Attached are committee minutes and reports and the top library management team notes. These notes from the latest management team meeting address each agenda item and constitute the official record of all decisions made by the top library management team. The notes reinforce or clarify reports made by department heads and team leaders to their respective unit groups. The GLOB is distributed to each library faculty and staff member, and posting copies are made available for student employees. The administrative assistant in Administrative Services has editorial responsibility for the GLOB and occasionally seeks advice from the dean on the suitability of specific items.

Committees

Committees are essential to the effective team management environment. They provide opportunities for horizontal and vertical communication among and between departments and are important for addressing library-wide functional issues. Functional committees are formed to coordinate activities regarding collection development, for example. Committees are appointed by the top library management team, the library faculty organization, or the dean.

In addition to the top library management team, the library faculty organization, and the library professional staff advisory council, the following standing committees are used at UNM:

Advisory Council on Automation
Type: Functional
Composition: Faculty or staff representatives from public and technical services departments.
Purpose: To review and recommend automation initiatives and changes.

Collection Development Coordinators
Type: Functional
Composition: Collection development officer and subject coordinators.
Purpose: To review major purchases, allocate funds, and write and review collection development policies and procedures.

Collection Development Selectors
Type: Functional
Composition: All selectors, collection development officer, and subject coordinators.
Purpose: To provide training for selectors, and to review collection development policies and procedures.

Committee on Committees
Type: Faculty
Composition: Three elected faculty members; and the secretary of the library faculty, the presiding officer, and the dean or designate as ex officio members.
Purpose: To make appointments to standing committees, to recommend appointments to search committees, and to present faculty issues to the library faculty.

Dean's Annual Progress Review Committee
Type: Administrative
Composition: One elected faculty member, one elected exempt staff member, one elected nonexempt staff member, and the head of administrative services as ex officio member.
Purpose: To review the input of faculty and staff for the dean's annual review and to summarize and report results.

Faculty Professional Enrichment Committee

Type: Faculty
Composition: Seven faculty members appointed by the committee on committees.
Purpose: To develop procedures for distribution of travel funds to faculty and to distribute such funds.

Library Employee Orientation Committee

Type: Functional
Composition: Seven to 12 faculty and staff members appointed by the committee on committees and the library professional staff advisory council; and a representative of the library personnel office as ex officio member.
Purpose: To facilitate orientation and familiarize new employees with the library.

Library Instruction Committee

Type: Functional
Composition: Faculty and staff members representing public services areas engaged in library instruction.
Purpose: To provide training for library instructors, share resources, and improve and coordinate library instruction.

LIBROS Advisory/Review Committee

Type: Functional
Composition: Faculty and staff members representing public and technical services areas and automation staff.
Purpose: To review and recommend changes to the online catalog.

Personnel Advisory/Review Committee

Type: Administrative
Composition: Two department heads, two nondepartment-head faculty, one exempt staff member, one nonexempt staff member; and the head of administrative services, the fiscal services manager, and the personnel coordinator as standing members. Appointed by the library management team.
Purpose: To review all personnel actions, including vacancies, reclassifications, and transfers, and to make personnel action recommendations to the library management team.

Public Services Discussion Group

Type: Functional

Composition: Faculty and staff members representing public services areas.

Purpose: To provide a forum for discussion of issues relating to the provision of services, and to provide training, share resources, and improve and coordinate reference services.

Research and Publications Committee

Type: Faculty

Composition: A minimum of six members, one of whom is a staff member. Appointed by the committee on committees and the library professional staff advisory council.

Purpose: To encourage and facilitate research and publication among library faculty, especially new faculty. To serve as a clearinghouse for information, and to sponsor workshops and seminars on research methodology and research in progress.

Sabbatical Review Committee

Type: Faculty

Composition: Five to seven library faculty members, the majority of whom shall be tenured. The chair shall be tenured.

Purpose: To review requests for sabbaticals and make recommendations to the dean.

Salary Equity Committee

Type: Administrative

Composition: Two department heads, two nondepartment-head faculty, one staff member, and the head of administrative services. Appointed by the library management team.

Purpose: To review all faculty and staff salaries on an annual basis for the purpose of identifying salary inequities, and to make recommendations to the dean and the library management team.

Staff Professional Enrichment Committee

Type: Administrative

Composition: Members of the library professional staff advisory council.

Purpose: To develop procedures for distribution of travel funds to staff and to distribute such funds.

Student Employment Advisory Committee

Type: Functional

Composition: Representatives from each department employing student assistants and the personnel coordinator.

Purpose: To provide a forum for discussion of issues relating to the supervision of student employees, and to provide training, share resources, and improve and coordinate student employment.

Technical Services Management Team

Type: Administrative

Composition: Representatives from each technical services department and unit and the associate dean.

Purpose: To serve as the management team for technical services units and departments. (Recommendations of the group are transmitted to the library management team for decision.) To provide a forum for discussion of issues relating to the operations of technical services.

Tenure and Promotion Committee

Type: Faculty

Composition: Seven elected library faculty members: five tenured and two untenured.

Purpose: To conduct promotion, code three, tenure, and post-tenure reviews of library faculty. To make recommendations to the dean.

In strict hierarchical organizations, committees are often viewed as a wasteful and inefficient means of operation. In the team management environment, committees involve faculty and staff in cooperative, participative decision making, and they greatly enhance communication across departmental and faculty-staff lines. Although possibly time-consuming and sometimes inefficient, the process is essentially important. Overall, committees are an effective means for improving communication and are essential in the team management environment.

Bibliography

Brown, Nancy A., and Jerry Malone. "The Bases and Uses of Power in a University Library." *Library Administration & Management* 2, no. 3 (June 1988): 141–44.

Drucker, Peter F. *Management: Tasks, Responsibilities, Practices*. New York: Harper & Row, 1974.

Euster, Joanne R. *Changing Patterns in Internal Communication in Large Academic Libraries*. Occasional paper no. 6. Washington, D.C.: ARL/OMS, 1981.

Fallon, William K., ed. *Leadership on the Job: Guides to Good Supervision*. New York: AMACOM, 1981.

Fuller, Robert M., and Stephen G. Franklin. *Supervision: Principles of Professional Management*. New York: Macmillan, 1982.

Ginzberg, Eli. *Understanding Human Resources*. Lanham, Md.: University Press of America, 1985.

Hawkins, Katherine W. "Implementing Team Management in the Modern Library." *Library Administration & Management* 3, no. 1 (winter 1989): 11–15.

Herzberg, Federick. *The Managerial Choice: To Be Efficient and to Be Human*. Homewood, Ill.: Dow Jones-Irwin, 1976.

Holllingsworth, A. T., and A. R. A. Al-Jafary. "Why Supervisors Don't Delegate and Employees Won't Accept Responsibility." *Supervisory Management* 28 (April 1983): 12–17.

Kanter, Rosabeth Moss. *The Change Masters: Innovations for Productivity in the American Corporation*. New York: Simon & Schuster, 1982.

Kaye, Kenneth. *Workplace Wars and How to End Them: Turning Personal Conflicts into Productive Teamwork*. New York: American Management Association, 1994.

Killian, Ray A. *Managers Must Lead!* Rev. ed. New York: AMACOM, 1979.

Lynch, Beverly P., ed. *Management Strategies for Libraries: A Basic Reader*. New York: Neal-Schuman, 1985.

Maccoby, Michael. *The Leader*. New York: Random House, 1981.

McCabe, Gerard B. *The Smaller Academic Library: A Management Handbook*. Westport, Conn.: Greenwood, 1988.

McGregor, Douglas. *The Human Side of Enterprise*. New York: McGraw-Hill, 1960.

———. *Leadership and Motivation: Essays*. Cambridge, Mass.: MIT Press, 1983.

Migneault, Robert LaLiberte. "Humanistic Management by Teamwork in Academic Libraries." *Library Administration & Management* 2, no. 3 (June 1988): 132–36.

Rosenbach, William E., and Robert L. Taylor. *Leadership: Challenges and Opportunities*. New York: Nichols, 1988.

Ross, Catherine, and Patricia Dewdney. *Communicating Professionally*. New York: Neal-Schuman, 1988.

Schuster, Frederick E. *Human Resource Management: Concepts, Cases and Readings*. 2d ed. Reston, Va.: Reston, 1985.

Siegel, Laurence, and Irving M. Lane. *Personnel and Organizational Psychology*. 2d ed. Homewood, Ill.: Richard W. Irwin, 1987.

Tichy, Noel M., and Mary Anne Devanna. *The Transformation Leader*. New York: John Wiley, 1986.

White, Herbert S. "Oh, Where Have All the Leaders Gone?" *Library Journal* 112, no. 16 (October 1, 1987): 68–69.

Zaleznik, Abraham. "Managers and Leaders: Are They Different?" *Harvard Business Review* 55, no. 3 (May/June 1977): 67–78.

•••••••Chapter 9

Supervision in the Team Management Environment

"Good management consists in showing average people how to do the work of superior people."
—John D. Rockefeller (1839–1937)

What Is a Supervisor?

Supervisors are found throughout library organizations. In the team management environment, supervisors include department heads, team leaders, unit heads, and rank-and-file staff with student supervisory responsibilities, and they serve multiple roles throughout the organization—those of supervisor, team leader, and team member.

The supervisor in an academic library occupies a unique and important position. The supervisor's job description likely includes the phrase "supervises librarians and staff members." In effect, the supervisor has responsibility for hiring, training, scheduling, assigning duties, disciplining, evaluating, counseling, and, above all, ensuring that those supervised contribute to the accomplishment of the unit or department's objectives and the objectives of the library. That brief phrase in the job description is often the most challenging and rewarding aspect of the job.

By definition, "anyone at the first level of management who has the responsibility for getting the 'hands-on-the-work' employees to carry out the plans and policies of higher level management is a supervisor."[1] The Taft-Hartley Act of 1947 defines a supervisor as "any individual having authority, in the interest of the employer, to hire, transfer, suspend, lay off, recall, promote, discharge, assign, reward, or discipline other employees, or responsibility to direct them, or to adjust their grievances, or effectively to recommend such action, if in connection with the foregoing the exercise of such authority is not of a merely routine or clerical nature, but requires the use of independent judgement."[2]

"Supervisor" is derived from a Latin term that means "look over." Historically, the supervisor was the person in charge of a group of workers and was a foreman or "fore man," at the lead of a group, setting the pace for the rest. Today's supervisor is a leader, one who watches over the work, and is a person with technical and professional skills.

In most library organizations, supervisors rise from the ranks and are usually employees with seniority who have worked at different jobs in the organization. Supervisors normally have more education than those they supervise. The supervisor either advances within the library to a position with supervisory responsibilities or is sometimes hired from the outside for a position that involves supervision.

The Multiple Roles of the Supervisor in Team Management

The supervisor must carry out hiring, training, scheduling, directing, disciplining, evaluating, and counseling responsibilities in a manner that is effective for the accomplishment of the unit's or department's mission. Because there is frequently more work than one person can accomplish, additional employees are needed. Therefore, the supervisor not only must accomplish work but also must get things done through others. It is the supervisor's responsibility to teach and apply supervisory techniques that will allow others to do things right. Every employee has different needs, skills, attitudes, and motivations. The supervisor needs to deal with each employee differently while dealing with all employees fairly. There is no universal technique that will work with every individual. What works today with one person may have no effect tomorrow, and what works on one may have a completely negative effect on another.

The supervisor's role as team leader requires a strong commitment to participative decision making, effective communication, and teamwork. The supervisor as team leader must possess all of the following personal qualities: energy, good health, leadership ability, interpersonal skills, knowledge of the job, initiative, dedication, dependability, and a positive attitude toward management. These qualities are desirable in any employee but are especially desirable in team leaders.

The supervisor must also be a good team member. As a team leader, the supervisor will be a member of a larger team—the department, or technical or public services, for example. Supervisors who are unit team leaders and also departmental team members should contribute to the success of the departmental team in the same manner expected of the unit's team members.

Can a supervisor avoid being a team leader or team member in the team management environment? Generally, no. The supervisor is normally expected to participate in a team—in the department set up as a team, as the department head who serves on the top management team, or in service on a task group established and run as a team. More than likely the supervisor will be a team member. Whether the unit or department is set up as a team may be left up to the supervisor or mandated by the organization. One thing that is absolutely required in the team management environment is regular staff meetings and some form of departmental report to other departments.

Could a department head survive in the team management environment without using the team approach in the department? Yes, but the likelihood of the department head being effective in the library's top management team would be small.

Moving from a Staff
to a Supervisory Position

The transition from rank-and-file worker to supervisor is difficult. The new supervisor must realize that "doing" and "supervising" require entirely different skills. In the team management environment, the supervisor must also deal with responsibilities as team leader and team member. The supervisor represents management to employees and employees to management. A delicate balance must be achieved if supervision is to be successful.

In the Humanistic Management by Teamwork environment, a tendency is to undermanage, allowing employees much flexibility in their jobs. In the effort to give employees ownership of their jobs and seek their participation in decision making, supervisors and team leaders can be viewed as relinquishing their management responsibilities. Attempts to regain overt control often result in charges of unfairness or even discrimination. Managers must be careful to maintain the balance of humanistic management by teamwork and authority.

Because most new supervisors are selected from among present staff in the library, it is important to remember that the move represents a significant change for everyone involved. Major differences between a subordinate and a supervisor include the following:

1. Perspective. Most employees are concerned primarily with doing a good job and planning how to get ahead. Supervisors, however, must keep the big picture in mind and consider the impact of their decisions on the department and the library.

2. Goals. A supervisor's primary concern is with meeting the organization's goals. This contrasts with employees' focus on meeting personal goals, such as becoming more skilled at their jobs.

3. Responsibilities. A supervisor must supervise and speak for a group of people in addition to completing technical and administrative tasks. A supervisor must also accept responsibility for decisions instead of criticizing others.

4. Satisfaction. Because a supervisor does less of the actual work, satisfaction comes from watching others succeed, rather than from the work itself.

5. Job skills. Becoming technically competent is important, but supervisors must also become proficient at communicating, delegating, planning, managing time, directing, motivating, and training others. Many of these are new skills that must be developed.

6. Relationships. If one is promoted to a supervisory position, new relationships must be developed with former peers, other supervisors, and the new boss. People quickly change the way they act toward the new supervisor, whether or not the supervisor changes behavior toward them.

Seven Transition Stages

The new supervisor does not normally make a successfull overnight transformation from thinking and behaving like a subordinate to thinking and behaving like a boss. Instead, the supervisor passes through several predictable stages. Although people seldom move neatly from one stage to the next, they generally experience all seven stages:

1. Immobilization. The person feels overwhelmed by change, typified by such thoughts as the following: "This job is a lot bigger than I thought. Everyone is making demands. How can I possibly do everything?"

2. Denial of change. This phase allows the individual time to regroup and fully comprehend the change: "This job is not so different from my other job. First I'll take care of this, and then I'll begin to work on that."

3. Depression. Awareness sets in regarding the magnitude of the changes that must be made in one's habits, customs, relationships, and so on: "Why did I ever leave my other job? I wish I could afford to quit. I hate my job!"

4. Acceptance of reality. Feelings of optimism return, and the person is ready to let go of the past: "Maybe this isn't so bad. Forget about that old job. I'm doing fine."

5. Testing. This is a time of trying out new behaviors and ways of coping with the new situation: "If I meet with staff every Thursday and try this schedule, I think I can manage."

6. Search for meanings. The person's concern shifts to trying to understand how and why things are different now: "Now I feel comfortable in this job. It is different but not really that bad."

7. Internalization. In this final stage, the person incorporates the new meanings into behavior. "I like my job and I'm good at what I do."

Problems of New Supervisors

One of the biggest problems facing new supervisors is lack of preparation for the job. An employee is often selected for promotion to a management position because of commendable performance as a library specialist. Such skills and abilities are often quite different than those needed from a supervisor. As a result, the new supervisor must develop new skills.

Organizations normally expect new supervisors to step into the job and immediately function as a supervisor. This expectation exists even though most organizations offer little help or support to them. Often, the new supervisor does not receive formal supervisory training until after six to 12 months on the job. The "sink or swim" philosophy is prevalent.

Finally, the new supervisor often lacks an immediate peer group. Former peers no longer regard the new supervisor as one of them. Other supervisors are hesitant to consider the new supervisor as part of their group until the new supervisor has demonstrated the ability to think and act like management. This leaves the new supervisor isolated at a time when support from others is often needed.

The team management environment can lessen the problems faced by new supervisors. Staff members promoted to supervisory positions will have prior experience as team members. As team members, they participate in decision making and see their team leaders in action. Thus they are exposed to both effective and ineffective supervisory techniques. The horizontal organization in the team management environment places the lowest-level staff closer to the top of the library management and encourages communication among departments, leading to new relationships among peers. The new supervisor or team leader can turn to those peers for advice and assistance. As a new supervisor, the individual will likely serve on another team, which increases the opportunities for support from other supervisors.

The new supervisor must be willing to learn, change, adapt, and ask for help when needed. Practicing supervisors must also recognize that it takes time for new supervisors to become effective and that they need help and support. Becoming a good supervisor is an ongoing process, and one should never stop learning.

Why Supervisors Fail

Whether in a team management environment or a hierarchy, new supervisors tend to make the following common mistakes:

1. Overcontrolling, believing that it is necessary to show everyone who is boss.

2. Undercontrolling, refusing to make decisions in an attempt to make everyone happy.

3. One-way communication, giving orders without listening, or just listening and providing no leadership.

4. Halfway delegation, delegating responsibility without the authority to act.

What Employees Do Not Like About Supervisors

One way to learn how to be a good supervisor is to think about the traits, actions, and skills of supervisors you have known and avoid any negative qualities in your own supervisory style. The following are some things employees do not like about their supervisors:

Traits of Supervisors

1. Too sensitive. Employees do not like to tiptoe around for fear of saying the wrong thing if the supervisor is in a bad mood or takes everything personally.

2. Indecisive. Indecisive supervisors can survive in an organization but will not win the support of employees.

3. Opinionated. Supervisors who will not listen to reasoning but always have their minds made up will find that employees soon stop making suggestions.

4. Autocratic. Supervisors must understand that if they do not allow employees to participate in decisions, a lot of good talent is wasted.

5. Uses vulgar language. Crude language is to be avoided at all costs.

6. Unstable. Employees should not have to guess which supervisor came to work that day. Unpredictable changes in the supervisor's personality cause problems.

7. Dishonest. Supervisors need to recognize the importance of honesty in the workplace and make it easy for employees to be honest.

Actions of Supervisors

1. Show favoritism. Employees resent it if another employee is given favorable treatment. Situations like this may lead to discrimination charges, though in most cases prejudice is not involved.

2. Do not listen. Good supervisors are anxious to hear what employees think about the job and try to get employees to talk. Nothing is more frustrating than to talk to a supervisor who does not listen.

3. Cannot accept bad news. Supervisors must be willing to listen to bad news and not punish the bearer. It will not take long for employees to realize that the supervisor wants to hear only good news, and that problems that need attention will be ignored.

4. Ridicule employees. Supervisors who ridicule or make sarcastic remarks to employees may not even realize they are doing it. Ridiculing an employee in front of peers is unforgivable. Supervisors must be aware of how their words affect employees.

5. Make uninformed decisions. Employees respect supervisors who make decisions based on information.

6. Do not trust employees. Supervisors must trust employees, and employees must be able to trust supervisors.

7. Make impossible promises. Employees know when supervisors make promises that cannot be kept. The supervisor's credibility is destroyed if this happens often.

8. Break reasonable promises. Employees also know when a supervisor's promises can be kept but are not. Supervisors must keep their word or be able to explain why a promise is not kept.

Practices of Supervisors

1. Poor time management. Supervisors with poor time management skills waste employees' time as well as their own.

2. Disorganization. Employees want supervisors who are organized and can get things done.

3. Failure to exert authority. Employees respect supervisors who know how to use their authority. Employees want a leader.

4. Poor planning. Supervisors who fail to plan waste employees' time. Poorly planned meetings, for example, are terrible time wasters.

5. Poor communication. Supervisors must develop good communication skills.

Pitfalls for Supervisors

Supervisory styles cover the full spectrum, from laissez-faire to authoritarian. The supervisor who lacks self-confidence or feels uncomfortable in the supervisory role tends to let the unit run itself. The dictatorial or authoritarian supervisor tends to oversupervise. Few good supervisors are found at either extreme; most often they are found in the middle of the spectrum. When a supervisor does not succeed, management must examine the specific situation to determine the exact reasons. It is possible that the failure can be traced to lack of support from the supervisor's superior or lack of training or encouragement. Most failures, however, can be attributed to one of the following six supervisory pitfalls:

1. Poor personal relations with employees, management, or other supervisors.

2. Lack of initiative or emotional stability on the part of the supervisor.

3. Unwillingness or inability to understand the management point of view.

4. Failure to spend the necessary effort or time to improve skills.

5. Lack of skill in planning and organizing the work of employees.

6. Unwillingness or inability to adjust to changing conditions.

Preparing to Become a Supervisor

Many people begin their library careers in public services or technical services positions without supervisory experience. The aspiring supervisor would do well to begin with the first function of management: planning. The following suggestions may aid the planning process:

1. Develop a career plan based on a realistic appraisal of your interests, aptitudes, and abilities.

2. If you are in a library with a career development program, take advantage of it.

3. Talk to several supervisors to learn more about what they do.

4. Talk to your supervisor to learn about opportunities for supervisory responsibilities.

5. Participate in supervisory and management training courses offered by the institution.

6. Complete college. Most supervisory positions require a bachelor's degree.

7. Remember that advancement depends on successful performance. Although successful performance of your job will not guarantee advancement and will not guarantee that you will be a successful supervisor, good supervisors advance from the ranks of good workers, not poor ones.

Summary

Many libraries underestimate the importance of the role of the supervisor. Librarians often do not receive the level of management training in library school that is required to manage complex organizations and usually develop their skills through trial and error. By understanding the importance of supervision and developing supervisory skills, the supervisor can make a valuable contribution to the success of the library.

The team leader in the team management environment must develop supervisory skills as well as team management skills. The team leader who lacks supervisory skills and is unwilling to develop those skills will not succeed in this environment. A poor supervisor will become evident in the team management environment more quickly than in a hierarchy because of the horizontal communication and the level of participation required for team activities. Nevertheless, the supervisor in the team management environment has more support and opportunities to learn and succeed with the assistance of team members and colleagues.

Bibliography

Abboud, Michael J., and Homer L. Richardson. "What Do Supervisors Want from Their Jobs?" *Personnel Journal* 51, no. 7 (July 1972): 308–12.

Bailey, Martha J. "Requirements for Middle Managerial Positions." *Special Libraries* 69 (September 1978): 323–31.

Baker, H. K., and S. R. Holmberg. "Stepping up to Supervision: Being Popular Isn't Enough." *Supervisory Management* 27 (January 1982): 12–18.

Baldwin, David A. *Supervising Student Employees in Academic Libraries*. Littleton, Colo.: Libraries Unlimited, 1991.

Bedeian, Arthur G. *Management*. Chicago: Dryden Press, 1986.

Benson, Carl A. "New Supervisors: From the Top of the Heap to the Bottom of the Heap." *Personnel Journal* 57 (April 1978): 176.

Bittel, Lester R. *What Every Supervisor Should Know*. New York: McGraw-Hill, 1980.

Bridges, William. *Transitions: Making Sense of Life's Changes*. Reading, Mass.: Addison-Wesley, 1980.

Carroll, Stephen J., and Dennis Gillen. "Are the Classical Management Functions Useful in Describing Managerial Work?" *Academy of Management Review* 12, no. 1 (January 1987): 38–51.

Certo, Samuel. *Principles of Modern Management*. 3d ed. Dubuque, Iowa: Wm. C. Brown, 1985.

Daughtrey, Anne Scott, and Betty Roper Ricks. *Contemporary Supervision: Managing People and Technology*. New York: McGraw-Hill, 1988.

Donnelly, James H., James L. Gibson, and John M. Ivancevich. *Fundamentals of Management*. 6th ed. Plano, Tex.: Business Publications, 1987.

Flamholtz, Eric G., and Yvonne Randle. *The Inner Game of Management: How to Make the Transition to a Managerial Role*. New York: AMACOM, 1987.

Fulmer, William E. "The Making of a Supervisor." *Personnel Journal* 56, no. 4 (March 1977): 140–43.

Gellerman, Saul W. "Supervision: Substance and Style." *Harvard Business Review* 54, no. 2 (March/April 1976): 89–99.

Hampton, David R. *Management*. 3d ed. New York: McGraw-Hill, 1986.

Hirschhorn, Larry. *Managing in the New Team Environment: Skills, Tools, and Methods*. Reading, Mass.: Addison-Wesley, 1991.

Ianconnetti, Joan, and Patrick O'Hare. *First-Time Manager*. New York: Macmillan, 1985.

Library Administration and Management Association, Middle Management Discussion Group. *You'll Manage: Becoming a Boss*. Chicago: Library Administration and Management Association, 1980.

Lynch, Beverly P. "The Role of Middle Managers in Libraries." *Advances in Librarianship* 6 (1976): 253–77.

Martell, Charles. "Automation, Quality of Work Life, and Middle Managers." Paper prepared for ALA/LAMA/Systems and Services Section/Management Practices Committee, New York, American Library Association Conference, June 28—July 3, 1986.

Masters, Lowell F. *Supervision for Successful Team Leadership: A Personal Analysis—The Questions and Answers You Need to Know*. Las Vegas, Nev.: Achievement Press International, 1992.

Mintzberg, Henry. "The Manager's Job: Folklore and Fact." *Harvard Business Review* 53, no. 4 (July/August 1975): 49–61.

Rees, Fran. *How to Lead Work Teams: Facilitation Skills*. San Diego, Calif.: Pfeiffer, 1991.

Sanborn, Mark. *Teambuilt, Making Teamwork Work*. New York: MasterMedia, 1992.

Sullivan, Maureen. *Librarians as Supervisors*. Workbook for ACRL Continuing Education Course CE 101. Chicago: American Library Association, 1982.

Van Fleet, James K. *The 22 Biggest Mistakes Managers Make and How to Correct Them*. West Nyack, N.Y.: Parker, 1973.

Weiss, W. H. *Supervisor's Standard Reference Handbook*. 2d ed. Englewood Cliffs, N.J.: Prentice-Hall, 1988.

Notes

1. Lester R. Bittel, *What Every Supervisor Should Know* (New York: McGraw-Hill, 1980), 3.

2. Labor Management Relations Act (PL101, 23 June 1947), *U.S. Statutes at Large* 61, pt. 1 (1947): 138.

•••••••• Chapter 10

Performance Appraisal in the
Team Management Environment

"Man cannot reach perfection in a hundred years;
he can fall in a day with time to spare."
—Chinese proverb

The Need for Performance Appraisal

In the team management environment, responsibility for the performance of rank-and-file individuals falls on the team leaders and the teams rather than at the top level of the library's administration. Therefore, the implementation of peer review and a performance appraisal system based on performance outcomes is an important component of the successful team management environment.

Performance appraisal is one of the most controversial activities carried out by organizations; however, it is impossible to make intelligent managerial decisions about employees without measuring their performance in some manner.

Formal performance appraisal is as old as the concept of management, and informal appraisal is as old as human history. All employees want and deserve to know what is being done well or not so well, how things can be done better, and how the job itself can be enhanced. However, performance appraisals can be debilitating for employees if done poorly. Persons who have received poor evaluations from supervisors, deserved or not, find that criticism is difficult to accept and that no matter how tough-skinned they think they are, the experience can be devastating.

Annual or formal performance appraisals should not be the only time that workers are told how they are doing, but a performance evaluation system, if done on schedule, guarantees that they are given regular feedback.

Purposes of Performance Appraisal

Performance appraisals have two basic purposes: employee evaluation and employee development. For most companies, evaluation for administrative purposes has determined the employee performance evaluation process. Appraisals of employee performance provide the basis for administrative decisions about promotions, demotions, terminations, transfers, and rewards. The development purpose has generally been secondary; however, evaluations used to improve performance on the job are becoming more common in the workplace.

Academic institutions generally view performance appraisal from a developmental viewpoint. There are three basic reasons for making effective performance appraisal of academic library employees:

1. To encourage good performance and to correct or discourage substandard performance. Good performers expect a reward, even if it is only praise. Employees who perform below standard should be made aware that continued poor performance will, at best, stand in the way of advancement. At worst, poor performance may lead to termination.

2. To satisfy employees' curiosity about how well they are doing. It is a fundamental curiosity of employees to want to know how well they are doing and how well they fit into the organization where they work. Although employees may dislike being judged, the need to know is very strong.

3. To provide a foundation for later judgments and decisions concerning employees: pay increases, promotions, transfers, or terminations. Supervisors are cautioned not to stress pay raises as the only part of the appraisal process. It is natural for an employee whose performance is rated good to expect a pay raise to follow. If the institution or library's compensation plan does not work that way, employees should not be told that their good work will necessarily result in a promotion or pay increase. It is important to explain to all employees just how the appraisal will be used.

Validity and Reliability

Good performance appraisals measure what they should; thus, they have validity. The outcomes are rational; that is, they have reliability. When a performance appraisal is valid, it measures what the supervisor and the supervisee want it to measure. Performance evaluations are not valid when they fail to measure performance-related behaviors and activities or when the performance measures are inappropriate to the job. When, for example, a supervisor allows a worker's hair length, style of clothing, or political beliefs to influence a given performance evaluation, the evaluation becomes problematic and invalid. These factors are not legitimate performance-related criteria and they have no value in a performance appraisal.

When a performance appraisal is reliable, it provides a useful measure of work performance. Supervisors must strive for consistency when evaluating employees. The most common types of reliability problems in performance appraisals are constant errors and random errors. Constant errors occur when all evaluations are in error to the same degree and are of the same kind. For example, a supervisor who rates all employees one point higher than their true rating is making a constant error. Who has not known a supervisor who rates all of the employees in a department as "excellent" when they should be rated as "good"? A random error occurs whenever a rating is unpredictably higher or lower than the individual should receive.

One way to deal with reliability errors is to use a corroborative technique. If one of the criteria to be evaluated is job speed, then there should be two or more questions on the rating form that relate to job speed. If the rating on one question shows that the worker is very slow, then the answers to the other questions relating to speed should match. If they do not, there is inconsistency. Multiple observations help supervisors correct erroneous evaluation responses and attain consistency.

Appraisal Formats

The library probably has an evaluation form developed internally or by the parent institution's personnel office. There are three basic types of performance appraisal forms: comparative, absolute, and outcome-based. The form most commonly used is the absolute format: a graphic rating scale or a narrative approach. With the comparative format, the supervisor evaluates employees in comparison to fellow employees. Comparative methods include ranking, paired comparisons, and forced choice. When absolute formats are used, the supervisor evaluates each employee's performance without comparing employees. Absolute methods include narrative, critical incidents, graphic rating scales, weighted checklists, and behaviorally anchored rating scales (BARS). If an outcome-based format is used, supervisors evaluate employees on the basis of performance outcomes. Common forms of outcome-based formats reflect standards of performance and management by objectives (MBO).

Peer Evaluation

The evaluation of employees is a managerial and supervisory responsibility that is not easily shared by the supervisor with others and should not be delegated. Peer evaluation, however, is one sharing technique that can be used to gain input for the appraisal of employee performance. Because co-workers have more first-hand continuous contact and opportunities to observe one another's performance, peer ratings can be quite valid. Peers judge performance from a perspective that is different from the supervisor's, and although subject to influence by positive or negative associations, peer comments may be keenly perceptive.

Peer evaluation deserves consideration by supervisors in organizations that have developed a climate of trust among co-workers and have noncompetitive reward systems. Peer evaluation is an effective tool for libraries using team management. Supervisors are cautioned that unless peer evaluation is an established part of the library's appraisal program, it should be avoided rather than arbitrarily invoked. Improper use of peer evaluation can cause enormous problems. It is often helpful, however, for a supervisor to gather input from persons the employee comes in contact with and to discuss opinions with the supervisor's supervisor in the preparation of employee evaluations.

Appraisal

The performance appraisal system developed at the UNM General Library evolved in stages. Before Humanistic Management by Teamwork was instituted, the appraisal system used narrative evaluations for library faculty and absolute forms for staff. The library dean was evaluated solely by central administration.

In 1986, at the urging of the new dean, Robert L. Migneault, the library faculty and staff developed upward evaluation procedures for the dean and associate dean, department heads, and supervisors. The procedures for each are described in the following sections.

Administrator Evaluation Procedure

The following procedure and assessment form were developed by the University of New Mexico General Library for upward performance review of the dean and associate dean:

University of New Mexico General Library
Dean and Associate Dean Annual Progress Review

1. The dean's annual progress review committee will be elected in March, to take office the following June.

   a. General Library faculty will elect one member.

   b. The library professional staff advisory committee will supervise the election of one member from the exempt staff.

   c. The library personnel specialist will supervise the election of one member from the nonexempt staff.

   d. The director of administrative services will serve as an ex officio member.

2. By September 1, the dean and associate dean will place a packet on reserve containing an up-to-date résumé, a statement of objectives for the coming year, a photocopy of the previous year's statement of objectives, the most recent biographical supplement, and a copy of the latest General Library annual report.

3. Assessment forms will be distributed to all library faculty and staff in September of each year by the director of administrative services.

4. Completed assessment forms must be signed and returned to the director of administrative services by the end of the third week in September. Anonymous input will not be accepted.

5. The assessment forms will be tallied by the deans' annual progress review committee.

6. The committee will present the results at an October meeting of the General Library faculty, to which the library professional staff advisory committee will be invited. The dean and associate dean will not be present during the discussion.

7. The committee will summarize the General Library faculty meeting discussion and write annual progress reviews for the dean and associate dean.

8. The committee will meet with the dean and associate dean to present the progress reviews.

9. The library management team will meet in closed session to write its annual progress reviews for the dean and associate dean. The dean and associate dean will not be present at this meeting.

10. The library management team will give copies of its annual progress reviews to the dean and associate dean.

11. The deans' annual progress review committee and the library management team will each prepare summaries of the reviews for the provost/vice president for academic affairs.

12. The director of administrative services will destroy the individual assessment forms one month after the library management team completes its reviews.

Assessment Form
Dean of Library Services/Associate Dean of Library Services

	Excellent (1)	Good (2)	Satisfactory (3)	Needs Work (4)	Un- satisfactory (5)	No Opinion (6)
Librarianship						
Leadership						
Administrative effectiveness						
Collegiality						
Communication skills						
Understanding new developments in librarianship						
Innovation						
Effective use of resources						
Sharing needed information						
Working relationships:						
University						
Administration						
University faculty						
Library faculty						
Library staff						
Promotion of good relations:						
With other libraries						
With professional groups						
Knowledge of library operations						
Accessibility						
Success in meeting personal goals						
Responsiveness to service needs						
Research						
Research, scholarship, and creative works						
Service						
To the university						
To the community						
To the profession						

If you have given this person a 1 or a 5 in any category, please explain:

Other comments: _____

Signature _____

Date _____

Department Head Evaluation Procedure

The following procedure and assessment form were developed by the University of New Mexico General Library for upward review of department heads and members of the top library management team:

University of New Mexico General Library
Department Head Annual Progress Review

1. For department heads, the annual progress review takes the place of the annual supervisory evaluation and the annual self-evaluation. The department head will be exempt from an annual progress review during the year he or she is being considered for code 3, tenure, promotion, or post-tenure review.

2. The director of administrative services will establish a schedule such that all department heads are evaluated each year. Ordinarily, one or two department head progress reviews will be scheduled each month.

3. The cycle of progress reviews will begin in July of each year.

4. One month prior to the date scheduled for the progress review, the department head will place a packet on reserve. The packet will contain an up-to-date résumé, a statement of objectives for the coming year, a photocopy of the previous year's statement of objectives, a personal assessment of the previous year's performance, and a copy of the latest departmental annual report.

5. The director of administrative services will send a cover memo and copy of the assessment form to all General Library faculty members and each staff member in the department whose head is being evaluated that month. In addition, the director of administrative services will place a notice in the GLOB informing all library staff that the packet is on reserve and inviting them to complete an assessment form that can be picked up in the library office.

6. Completed assessment forms must be signed and returned to the associate dean. Anonymous input will not be accepted.

7. During the month that the packet is on reserve, the dean or associate dean will schedule a meeting with the appropriate department to discuss the department head's performance. Individuals may also schedule private meetings with the dean or associate dean for that purpose.

8. The associate dean will prepare a summary of the assessments received, to be presented on the scheduled date at a closed meeting of the library management team. The person being evaluated will not be present.

9. The library management team will designate one of its members to write a progress review based on the team's assessment.

10. The dean or associate dean will schedule a meeting with the department head being evaluated to present and discuss the progress review. The department head will receive a numerical summary of the responses received on the assessment forms, as well as a copy of the written progress review.

11. A copy of the progress review will be placed in the individual's personnel file.

12. The associate dean will present a summary of the evaluation at the next regular General Library faculty meeting.

13. The associate dean will meet with the staff of the department whose head was reviewed and present a summary of the evaluation.

14. The director of administrative services will destroy the individual assessment forms one month after the review process is completed.

Assessment Form
Library Department Heads

This is the only evaluation this department head is scheduled to receive this year. It will be used to assess annual progress toward tenure or post-tenure, to review supervisory performance, to evaluate contributions as a member of the library management team, and to determine allocation of merit pay. It is designed to be used by both faculty and staff. Because this one form serves so many purposes, no one evaluator is going to be able to comment on all the different categories listed here. Please check "No Opinion" for those items you have not been in a position to observe.

	Excellent (1)	Good (2)	Satisfactory (3)	Needs Work (4)	Un- satisfactory (5)	No Opinion (6)
Performance As a Department Head						
Leadership						
Competence as a manager						
Supervisory skills						
Understanding new developments						
Innovation						
Relations with community						
In-depth knowledge of departmental operations						
Promoting faculty and staff development						
Encouraging innovation and initiative						
Promotion of positive work environment:						
Motivates workers						

	Excellent (1)	Good (2)	Satisfactory (3)	Needs Work (4)	Un-satisfactory (5)	No Opinion (6)
Gives recognition						
Communicates expectations						
Distributes needed information						
Accessibility						
Responsiveness to service needs						

Performance As a Faculty Member

Librarianship						
Collegiality						
Understanding new developments						
Relations within university						
Knowledge of library operations						
Success in meeting stated objectives						
Research, scholarship, and creative works						
Service:						
To the university						
To the community						
To the profession						

Performance As an LMT Member

Leadership						
Understanding new developments						
Collegiality						
Represents department concerns to LMT, dean						
Distribution of needed information						
Effective advocacy in team environment						
Positive contribution to the team						

If you have given this person a 1 or a 5 in any category, please explain:

Other comments: _____

Signature _____

Date _____

Supervisor Evaluation Procedure

The following procedure and assessment form were developed by the University of New Mexico General Library for review of supervisors:

University of New Mexico
General Library Supervisor Assessment

Rationale

1. Evaluations of supervisors by staff are desirable and essential to the effective operation of the library.

2. Evaluations provide supervisors with an assessment of the quality of their performance.

3. Evaluations strengthen communication and understanding between supervisors and their staff.

Responsibility for Administration

1. The assessment form and instructions will be mailed by the administrative services office to all department heads in January of each year.

2. A notice will be placed in the GLOB informing the staff of the evaluation process.

3. The department head will initiate staff evaluations for supervisors either before each staff supervisor's annual review or at any other time the department head considers appropriate. The department head is advised to conduct the evaluation in conjunction with the annual review and in time for the annual merit review in March.

Procedure

1. Employees have the option of evaluating their supervisor by writing a signed memo, completing an assessment, or meeting with their supervisor's supervisor. The criteria outlined on the assessment form can be used as criteria for a memo.

2. The evaluations will be incorporated into the annual review of the supervisor. At the completion of the evaluation process, all written evaluations and any notes taken during oral evaluations will be destroyed.

Assessment Form
Supervisor

	Excellent (1)	Good (2)	Satisfactory (3)	Needs Work (4)	Un-satisfactory (5)	No Opinion (6)

Performs Supervisory Functions

Keeps employees informed						
Gives clear work assignments						
Is accessible						
Provides feedback						
Makes expectations known						
Is tactful and considerate						
Promotes team environment						
Promotes good working relationships						
Communicates employees' concerns						
Delegates authority						
Provides training of new employees						
Plans, paces, and organizes work						

Comments:

Develops Innovative Procedures

Is receptive to new ideas						
Is receptive to questions						
Encourages initiative and innovation						

Comments:

Maintains Positive Work Environment

Recognizes contributions						
Motivates workers						
Provides relaxed yet efficient work atmosphere						
Encourages staff development						

Comments:

	Excellent (1)	Good (2)	Satisfactory (3)	Needs Work (4)	Un-satisfactory (5)	No Opinion (6)

Knows Operations of Department

	Excellent	Good	Satisfactory	Needs Work	Un-satisfactory	No Opinion
Understands employee workload						
Is aware of unit operations						
Understands organizational structure						
Is alert to potential problems						
Understands new developments						

Comments:

Work Habits

	Excellent	Good	Satisfactory	Needs Work	Un-satisfactory	No Opinion
Acknowledges own limitations and mistakes						
Maintains a positive work attitude						
Uses time efficiently and effectively						
Sets a good example						

Comments:

Signature _____

Date _____

Outcome-Based Appraisal

The evaluation procedures for administrators, department heads, and supervisors at UNM General Library were quite successful, but with the additional peer reviews for faculty probationary, promotion, and tenure decisions, the entire process was time-consuming. It seemed that there were too many evaluations. A performance evaluation review committee, formed to streamline the appraisal process, recommended an outcome-based appraisal procedure for faculty. After the library faculty adopted the procedure, the library professional staff advisory committee developed a similar process for staff. These procedures have remained in place for all faculty and staff except for the dean and associate dean. The procedures (covered earlier) for the upward review of the dean and associate dean remain in force.

The best-known forms of outcome-based methods are standards of performance and management by objectives (MBO). Standards of performance involves comparing performance to a list of standards established through negotiation between the worker and the supervisor. The list of standards comprises conditions that must be met if the job is considered to have been done well.

MBO is a method of evaluation that focuses on specific objectives or goals established by negotiation between the employee and the supervisor. The employee is judged on how well those objectives are met.

The procedures in place at UNMGL are based on standards of performance. The procedure for annual assessment of faculty begins below; the procedure for annual assessment of staff begins on page 154; the procedure for preparing the statement of job responsibilities (which are the basis for preparing objectives for annual assessment of faculty and staff) begins on page 156.

University of New Mexico General Library
Annual Assessment of UNMGL Faculty

Summary

The purpose of the annual evaluation of all UNMGL faculty is to assess the performance of the individual faculty member. An assessment will be conducted in February to review job performance during the previous calendar year. The basis of the review will be a negotiated list of job objectives that expands on the faculty member's individual statement of job responsibilities and that includes activities in the areas of job performance, research and scholarship, and service. An open, ongoing dialog between the faculty member and the supervisor is critical to the success of the assessment process. The assessment will include a merit recommendation. The assessment process is complemented by the activities of the mentor program and the research and publication committee. A separate process, tenured review of untenured faculty, provides feedback on progress toward code 3 (midway to the tenure review), tenure, and promotion.

Purpose

- To assess job performance
- To measure employee's contribution to the library
- To identify goals for evaluating job performance
- To determine merit recommendations
- To provide feedback on employee's performance
- To determine training and development needs

- To take into account individual differences in job responsibilities and in professional abilities

Procedural Guidelines

- By the end of January: Assessments of supervisors completed. All library staff and faculty are encouraged to participate in the performance assessment of supervisors by submitting their comments to the appropriate person (step 1).

- By the beginning of February: Code 1, 2, 4, and 5 library faculty will turn in their assessment folders (step 4).

- By the third week of February: Completion of the untenured faculty progress review (step 4).

- By the end of February: Completion of the annual assessment (step 2).

- By the end of March: Completion of list of objectives for the new calendar year (step 3).

1. Supervisor evaluations: The annual performance evaluation includes a supervisor review component. In January, all faculty and staff will receive a supervisor assessment form. All staff and faculty are encouraged to complete these forms for supervisors and department heads. The evaluation forms are forwarded to the appropriate department head, or in the case of a department head evaluation, to the dean. The results of the supervisor evaluation are incorporated into the annual assessment document.

2. Assessment document: During February and March each year, two performance evaluation documents will be prepared. The first document is an assessment of the previous year's performance. This assessment should be completed by February 28. Success in meeting specific negotiated objectives is the basis of the assessment document. The second document is a negotiated list of objectives for the current calendar year. The list of objectives should be established by March 31. See section 3.

In February, the supervisor and faculty member will review the negotiated list of objectives from the previous calendar year. At this meeting, the faculty member will describe to what extent the objectives have been met. In case an objective was not met, the faculty member has the opportunity to explain why. The faculty member can also identify other accomplishments that were not listed on the previous year's list of objectives. A written self-evaluation also may be prepared by the faculty member. The performance evaluation process recognizes that job opportunities may occur during the year that were not included on the previous year's list.

During the meeting, the supervisor and faculty member will prepare an assessment document outlining the degree of success in achieving the stated objectives. As described in the General Library merit criteria document, the supervisor will assign a numerical value to each of the three assessment areas: job performance, research and scholarship, and service.

Based on the discussion with the faculty member, the supervisor will prepare a final copy of the assessment document by February 28.

A copy will be given to the faculty member, and the assessment presented to the library management team during merit discussions. Merit points may be adjusted during the library management team discussion.

If the supervisor and the faculty member cannot come to an agreement about a performance assessment, a mediation committee will be formed at the request of the faculty member. This committee will consist of individuals who are familiar with the faculty member's performance. The committee members will be selected by the supervisor and the faculty member. The mediation committee will prepare its own assessment document after meeting with the supervisor and the faculty member. The committee will then present its document to the faculty member and the supervisor. Based on the assessment document submitted by the mediation committee, the supervisor may revise his or her assessment document. The committee's document will be attached to the supervisor's report. If the disagreement cannot be resolved by the mediation committee, other options can be explored with the director of administrative services.

3. Negotiated list of objectives: After the supervisor and the faculty member have discussed the assessment document, a second meeting will be arranged to discuss the coming year's objectives. The list of objectives is a negotiated product. The objectives should be specific. It is important that the supervisor and the faculty member mutually understand each objective and how the objective will be accomplished and measured. It is the supervisor's responsibility to include objectives reflecting the library's goals. It is the faculty member's responsibility to identify objectives that are appropriate for his or her statement of job responsibilities. Objectives may be revised at any time during the year in consultation with the supervisor and/or department head. The faculty member will provide a typed copy of the negotiated list of objectives to the supervisor by March 31. The list of objectives is normally limited to one page.

4. Untenured faculty progress review by tenured faculty: By February 1, each untenured faculty member in code years 1, 2, 4, and 5 will provide the director of administrative services with an annual assessment folder to be placed in the dean's office. The folder will consist of the following materials:

   a. A one-page statement of job responsibilities for the previous year.

   b. A one-page list of job objectives for the previous year.

   c. A one-page progress report based on the above two documents.

   d. The UNM supplement to the biographical record for the previous year.

   e. An offprint or similar copy of any new published or creative work or evidence of work in progress from the previous year.

   f. A current résumé.

   g. Previous progress reports.

The presiding officer of the library faculty will call and conduct the tenured faculty meetings. A presenter will be selected for each of the code 1, 2, 4, and 5 faculty members. Each presenter will become acquainted with the person's assessment folder. Tenured faculty unfamiliar with a person's performance may also wish to consult the folder. The presenter for each untenured faculty member will make a brief and objective presentation on librarianship, scholarship and research, and service performance, based on the assessment folder information. The tenured faculty will discuss each untenured faculty member's performance until a consensus is reached on progress toward tenure. Sponsors and department head evaluators, whether tenured or not, are expected to attend the appropriate reviews. The dean of library services shall attend all review discussions. Members present will share the task of preparing progress reports based on the discussions. All reports will share a common structured format for consistency and ease of interpretation. The entire review process must be completed by the third week of February.

Copies of each progress report will be distributed to the individual, the department head evaluator, the dean of library services, the sponsor, and the library personnel file. The progress reports will become part of the individual's code 3 and tenure packets.

5. Tenured faculty: Tenured faculty shall have the written annual assessment as described in section 1 (supervisor evaluations) if applicable, and section 2 (assessment document) of this policy. The annual assessment folder shall include the following: statement of job responsibilities, list of job objectives, self-assessment, annual performance evaluation, current résumé, and biographical supplement. It shall be the responsibility of the director of administrative services to assure that the evaluations are completed.

6. Faculty department heads: The annual assessment as described in section 1 (supervisor evaluations) and section 2 (assessment document) of this policy must be completed and sent to the associate dean of library services. Refer to the schedule in section 1 for completion dates. These additional steps apply to all department heads:

   a. The associate dean of library services (or designee) may arrange for meetings of the dean or associate dean or both with the staff of each department to discuss the department head's annual assessment.

   b. The associate dean of library services (or designee) shall arrange for meetings of each department head with the dean or associate dean or both to discuss the assessment and the next year's objectives.

7. Dean and associate dean evaluations: The procedures in the existing policy, dean and associate dean annual progress review, will be followed.

University of New Mexico General Library
Annual Assessment of UNMGL Staff

Summary

The purpose of the annual evaluation of all UNMGL staff is to assess the performance of the individual staff member. An assessment will be conducted in February to review job performance during the previous calendar year. The basis of the review will be a negotiated list of job objectives that expands on the staff member's individual statement of job responsibilities. During the year, an open, ongoing dialog between the staff member and the supervisor is critical to the success of the assessment process. The assessment will include a merit recommendation for exempt staff.

Purpose

- To assess job performance and orient the employee toward future performance.

- To acknowledge the employee's contribution to the library.

- To identify goals for evaluating job performance.

- To address training and development needs.

- To take into account individual differences in job responsibilities and in professional abilities.

- To give employees the opportunity to use their insight into the goals and performance of their own job.

- To determine merit recommendations for exempt staff.

- To provide feedback on the employee's performance.

Procedural Guidelines

1. Assessment document: In February, the supervisor and staff member will review the negotiated list of objectives from the previous calendar year. At this meeting, the staff member will describe to what extent the objectives have been met. In case an objective was not met, the staff member has the opportunity to explain why. The staff member can also identify other accomplishments that were not listed on the previous year's list of objectives. A written self-evaluation also may be prepared by the staff member. The performance evaluation process recognizes that job opportunities may occur during the year that were not included on the previous year's list.

During the meeting, the supervisor and staff member prepare an assessment document outlining the degree of success in achieving the stated objectives. Some suggestions for the supervisor to consider in evaluating the fulfillment of objectives established for the previous year are listed below. Because job responsibilities differ, care should be taken to apply these criteria as they relate to the staff member's job responsibilities and objectives:

- Development and implementation of techniques or methods that result in significant improvements in services or operations in the library.

- Ability to perform functions in a creative and innovative fashion or to introduce innovative procedures, techniques, etc., or both.

- Productivity combined with quality.

- Contribution of job performance to the overall performance and enhancement of the unit.

- Evaluation of the staff member based on feedback from library patrons, colleagues, and library employees.

- Based on the discussion with the staff member, the supervisor will prepare a final copy of the assessment document by March 1. A copy will be given to the staff member and the assessment presented to the library management team by the appropriate department head.

2. Mediation: If the supervisor and the staff member cannot come to an agreement about a performance assessment, the director of administrative services or the staff member's department head or both will mediate. Based on this mediation, the supervisor may revise the assessment document. If the disagreement cannot be resolved by mediation, a recommendation is made to the dean by the director of administrative services, with the exception of administrative services staff, for which the associate dean will act as mediator.

3. Negotiated list of objectives: After the supervisor and the staff member have discussed the assessment document, a second meeting will be arranged to discuss the coming year's objectives. The list of objectives is a negotiated product. The objectives should be specific. It is important that the supervisor and the staff member mutually understand each objective and how the objective will be accomplished and measured. It is the supervisor's responsibility to include objectives reflecting the library's goals. It is the staff member's responsibility to identify objectives that are appropriate for the person's statement of job responsibilities. Objectives may be revised at any time during the year in consultation with the supervisor or department head or both. The staff member will provide a typed copy of the list of negotiated objectives to the supervisor by March 31. The list of objectives is normally limited to one page.

4. Supervisor evaluations: The annual performance evaluation includes a supervisor review component. In January, all staff and faculty will receive a supervisor assessment form. All staff and faculty are encouraged to complete these forms for their supervisor or department head or both. The evaluation forms are forwarded to the appropriate department head, or in the case of a department head evaluation, to the associate dean. The results of the supervisor evaluation are incorporated into the annual assessment document. The supervisor should not reveal directly or indirectly the identity of the evaluator.

University of New Mexico
General Library Instructions for
Preparing the Statement of Job Responsibilities

The following guidelines are to be used in preparing the statement of job responsibilities. Note that the emphasis in the preparation is on brevity and clarity.

1. The sentence structure for writing job responsibilities should be verb, object, then explanatory phrase. The implied subject

of each of these sentences is the incumbent occupying the job, for example: "plans and conducts bibliographic instruction sessions for humanities classes on request" and "develops annual operating budgets for the department." The explanatory phrase should demonstrate why, how, where, or how often the task or duty is performed. This phrase adds meaning and is essential.

2. The present tense is to be used throughout the statement of job responsibilities.

3. Avoid words that are subject to varying interpretations, such as some, great, or occasionally.

4. Avoid proprietary names such as WordPerfect, LOTUS, and dBase. These references are subject to change.

5. Avoid sexist terminology. Construct statements in such a way that gender pronouns are not required.

6. Describe the position as it is now and not as it will exist sometime in the future.

7. Statements of job responsibilities are to be kept to one page if possible.

Statements of job responsibilities are not intended to be and should not be construed to be exhaustive lists of all responsibilities, skills, efforts, or working conditions associated with the position described. Instead, the statement of job responsibilities is intended to be an accurate reflection of principal job elements. The following disclaimer should be added at the end of all statements of job responsibilities:

Disclaimer: The above statement reflects the general duties considered necessary to describe the principal activities of the job identified and shall not be considered inclusive of all work requirements that may be inherent in the position.

The statement of job responsibilities differs from a job description in that it does not include the position's educational and experience requirements.

Why Use Outcome-Based Appraisals?

The statement of job responsibilities clearly defines the basic components of the job for the supervisor and the employee and provides a definitive list of job duties. The objectives define what the employee would like to accomplish and what the supervisor wants to see accomplished during the evaluation year. When the employee and the supervisor negotiate a list of objectives for the coming year, they establish what will be evaluated at year's end. The supervisor may include objectives that call for corrective action by the employee during the year. Discussions of the objectives when they are set and throughout the year become the joint responsibility of both parties. The shared responsibility allows the employee to approach the supervisor to discuss the job and to revise objectives and negotiate new objectives during the year. This eliminates the problem of the supervisor evaluating the employee on activities other than those previously agreed to. The appraisal itself becomes an evaluation of the objectives and how well they were met. This approach makes it very difficult for the supervisor to evaluate the employee's personality, a mistake that causes most of the problems in evaluations and is devastating to employee self-image.

Appraisal Errors

Some of the more common errors committed by evaluators also must be guarded against in outcome-based appraisals:

1. Personal bias: Unfairly judging members of different races, religions, genders, or national origins.

2. The halo effect: Letting appraisal of one factor affect appraisal of all other factors.

3. Central tendency: Rating most workers as average, thus making no distinctions between good and poor performers.

4. Harshness: Rating everyone at the low end of the scale.

5. Leniency: Rating everyone at the high end of the scale.

6. Similarity: Rating people who are like the evaluator higher than people who are different from the evaluator.

7. Recent events: Allowing recent events to affect judgment of the person's performance over the entire evaluation period.

8. Seniority: Unfairly judging workers according to length of time on the job.

9. Acquaintanceship: Letting how well the evaluator knows the employee affect the appraisal.

Making Nondiscriminatory Appraisals

In our litigious society, more and more employers are being sued by employees and former employees; therefore, it is important to be aware of what is legal and permissible in appraising employee performance. The key to making nondiscriminatory appraisals is quite simple: Evaluate all employees on the basis of job performance only, be consistent in application, and apply criteria objectively to all employees. Evaluating employees on the basis of job performance means judging them only on the way they do their jobs without regard to their age, race, sex, religion, national origin, age, or other illegal factors. It also means putting aside any personal likes or dislikes. Outcome-based evaluation focuses on the standards of performance (the list of objectives) and not on personality, lessening the possibility of discrimination.

Confidentiality of Appraisals

With the outcome-based appraisal system in the team management environment, lists of objectives can be shared with the team, in part to make sure all activities are covered and to inform the team of what its members are doing or not doing. The appraisals based on shared objectives, however, should be confidential. The appraisal of one employee should never be discussed with other employees. The supervisor cannot control what employees discuss with one another, but the supervisor should never be the source of information for those discussions. Supervisors should avoid comparing employees when conducting appraisal meetings. And supervisors should make it clear to each employee that all ratings and appraisals are confidential.

Good Evaluations Do Not Always Result in Advancement

The employee who consistently gets positive appraisals often finds it hard to accept the fact that it is not possible to move up in a seniority-based system until the person ahead gets promoted or quits. In a seniority-based system, everyone on the team must understand how seniority works. If the compensation system is not tied directly to the appraisal system, employees should be appropriately informed. They should be informed on what the appraisal process is all about. If merit increases are possible, supervisors should describe the process and explain possibilities to employees. If longevity is the deciding factor in raises, employees should be informed of this. Misconceptions about how the performance appraisals are used must be cleared up so that everyone has a common understanding of the process. Employees should also know what happens to the appraisal forms and how they may be used. Who has access to them? A written library policy is recommended. Does the library give references on former employees and are the appraisal forms used? This, too, should be covered by library policy.

Follow-Up to the Appraisal

The appraisal is done, the meeting has been held, and the forms have been filed. Is that all there is? No, appraisal is not something that is done today and forgotten tomorrow. For appraisals to be of value, the supervisor should do the following after the appraisal meeting:

1. Keep promises. The supervisor who has agreed to do something during the appraisal meeting should do it. If, for example, the supervisor promised to show the employee data referred to in the meeting, the supervisor should follow through.

2. Implement an employee development plan. If the supervisor said the employee needs training in an area, the supervisor should make arrangements to provide that training. The supervisor should locate courses, workshops, or seminars that will provide the needed training, or talk to the individual who will train the employee. The worker should be informed about those arrangements.

3. Keep in touch. The supervisor should continue to show interest in the development of the employee by monitoring the employee's performance, giving credit for improvement and pointing out deficiencies.

Frequently, supervisors and employees assume too much. Supervisors assume that employees know exactly what is expected of them and that they know how well they are doing. Employees assume that the work is being performed to the supervisor's satisfaction. The "no news is good news" syndrome operates in many libraries until tempers flare, feelings are hurt, and productivity declines. Annual or semiannual performance appraisals are certainly useful in alleviating the problem, but performance appraisals should be an ongoing activity. There should be no surprises at formal appraisal time if supervisors give employees frequent feedback on their performance, discuss their work, and talk regularly with them. The performance appraisal itself ceases to be a confrontational or traumatic experience for the supervisor or the employee if the supervisor shows genuine interest and humanistic concern on a regular basis.

Bibliography

Allan, Ann, and Kathy J. Reynolds. "Performance Problems: A Model for Analysis and Resolution." *Journal of Academic Librarianship* 9 (May 1983): 83–89.

Association of Research Libraries, Office of Management Studies. *Performance Appraisal in Reference Services.* Washington, D.C.: Association of Research Libraries, 1987.

———. *Performance Appraisal in Research Libraries.* Washington, D.C.: Association of Research Libraries, 1988.

Berkner, Dimity S. "Library Staff Development Through Performance Appraisal." *College & Research Libraries* 40, no. 4 (July 1979): 335–44.

Creth, Sheila. *Performance Evaluation: A Goals-Based Approach*. Chicago: Association of College and Research Libraries, 1984.

DeProspo, Ernest R. "Personnel Evaluation as an Impetus to Growth." *Library Trends* 20, no. 1 (July 1971): 60–70.

Gibbs, Sally E. "Staff Appraisal." In *Handbook of Library Training Practice*, edited by Ray Prytherch, 61–81. Brookfield, Vt.: Gower, 1986.

Hilton, R. C. "Performance Evaluation of Library Personnel." *Special Libraries* 69 (November 1978): 429–34.

Hodge, Stanley P. "Performance Appraisals: Developing a Sound Legal and Managerial System." *College & Research Libraries* 44, no. 4 (July 1983): 235–44.

Kroll, H. R. "Beyond Evaluation: Performance Appraisal as a Planning and Motivational Tool in Libraries." *Journal of Academic Librarianship* 9 (March 1983): 27–32.

Library Administration and Management Association, Personnel Administration Section, Staff Development Committee. *Personnel Performance Appraisal: A Guide for Libraries*. Chicago: Library Administration and Management Association, 1979.

Lindsey, Jonathan A. "The Human Dimension in Performance Appraisal." *North Carolina Libraries* 42, no. 1 (spring 1984): 5–7.

———. *Performance Evaluation: A Management Basic for Librarians*. Phoenix, Ariz.: Oryx Press, 1987.

Lubans, John. "Performance Evaluation: Worth the Cost?" *North Carolina Libraries* 42, no. 1 (spring 1984): 15–17.

Mager, Robert F., and Peter Pipe. *Analyzing Performance Problems, or: You Really Oughta Wanna*. 2d ed. Belmont, Calif.: Wadsworth, 1987.

McGregor, Douglas. "An Uneasy Look at Performance Appraisal." *Harvard Business Review* 25, no. 2 (May/June 1957): 89–94.

Pinzelik, Barbara P. "A Library Middle Manager Looks at Performance Appraisal." In *Energies for Transition, Proceedings of the Fourth National Conference of ACRL*, edited by Danuta A. Nitecki, 141–45. Chicago: Association of College and Research Libraries, 1986.

Reneker, Maxine H. "Performance Appraisal in Libraries: Purpose and Techniques." In *Personnel Administration in Libraries*, edited by Sheila Creth and Frederick Duda, 227–89. New York: Neal-Schuman, 1981.

Rice, B. "Performance Appraisal: The Job Nobody Likes." *Psychology Today* 19 (September 1985): 30–36.

Vincelette, J. P. "Improving Performance Appraisal in Libraries." *Library and Information Science Research* 6 (April 1984): 191–203.

Yarbrough, Larry N. "Performance Appraisal in Academic and Research Libraries." *ARL Management Supplement* 3 (May 1975): 1–6.

• • • • • • • •Chapter 11

The Practitioner's Viewpoint

"If you can talk about and do it,
then, buddy, you ain't braggin'!"
—Jay Hanna "Dizzy" Dean (1911–1974)

The authors of this book have strived to give readers an understanding of what teamwork is, how teamwork can be effectively used in the academic library setting, and specific examples of how management by teamwork can be implemented. To conclude, the authors feel it would be useful and instructive to provide answers to a series of questions that shed more light on the Humanistic Team Management philosophy and practice. Robert L. Migneault, Professor and Dean of Library Services, is the architect of Humanistic Management by Teamwork (HMBT) at the University of New Mexico General Library (UNMGL). Dean Migneault has developed an organization that is unique in the United States. His description of Humanistic Management by Teamwork provides insights on how this management approach is different from the traditional hierarchy.

Humanistic Foundations

 What exactly is HMBT and what made you introduce it at the University of New Mexico?

When I became dean of library services at the University of New Mexico, I wanted agreement on how to manage the General Library. Once I had convinced myself that HMBT had real possibilities as a managerial system, I described the basic elements of the philosophy and practice to UNMGL managers and supervisors. After several discussions, we decided that HMBT would be an acceptable alternative for the General Library. The genesis of HMBT as a concept was in the assessment of the library's mission, of the setting and environment in which the mission was to be carried out, and of the resources and means available.

163

What was/is your assessment of the library's mission, setting and environment, and resources and means?

UNMGL's mission is consistent with the missions of academic libraries throughout the nation. UNMGL exists primarily to support and enhance its parent body's academic, research, and service activities. UNMGL is viewed as a service organization for the state's flagship institution of higher learning. The setting may best be described as southwestern, academic, and actively research-oriented. The environment is strongly characterized by its unique cultural identity, diversity, emerging values regarding democratization and empowerment, societal and technological change, and no small amount of ambiguity in the workplace. Library resources are finite, never enough, and always in a state of endangerment. The means by which UNMGL can operate are best represented by people. Clearly, people should be the priority when it comes to academic library management.

 In effecting HMBT, how do people and the library's mission come together?

People and the library's mission come together at two interlocking levels, philosophical and practical. Philosophically speaking, mission holds the first rank of importance. In effecting HMBT, mission must be given the fundamental consideration—for without mission (in theory), there is little, if any, purpose to a given activity, and people would not be a subject for HMBT. Although mission is the "prime mover," the people who are expected to fulfill the mission must be given priority attention. In the abstract, the academic library's mission has centrality because it connects meaningfully with universal ideals, such as learning and truth. In concrete terms, the academic library's mission has centrality because it connects meaningfully with practical realities, such as jobs and salaries. HMBT embodies the basic assumption that, whenever an employee acts, he or she expresses not only his or her "own" humanity, but also effectively expresses a humanity intrinsic to "everyone." HMBT requires such an assumption for existential reasons, at the heart of which is the importance placed on "meaning." HMBT espouses that employees must collectively fulfill the library's mission to bring to their work the meaning that is so necessary if good job performance is to be properly sustained.

In HMBT, how does humanistic management compare with "being humane"?

HMBT devotes significant effort to promoting an attitude of concern for human beings and their values, capacities, and achievements. HMBT regards "being humane"—being charitable, good-natured, and kindhearted—as inherently worthwhile, desirable, and useful in the workplace. However, HMBT does not expect its practitioners to be overly or irresponsibly eleemosynary (charitable) in their behavior. For obvious reasons, administrators, managers, and supervisors are not expected to give away the store. HMBT is very much pro-management. It is designed for encouraging a high level of organizational performance. HMBT guides individual human values and traits—humanistically—to advance the organization as a whole.

 What is "humanistic guiding" and how does it fit within the context of HMBT?

[According to Migneault, who coined the term] Humanistic guiding is the careful and caring orchestration of human values and traits of individuals for organizational purposes. In other words, humanistic guiding is a managerial means by which individual human values and traits are ethically ushered for collectively advancing the organization as a whole. Humanistic guiding recognizes the fact that employees are competent, conscientious, creative, dependable, fair, hardworking, honest, imaginative, knowledgeable, pleasant, productive, responsible, talented, and trustworthy. The nuances of humanistic guiding favor managerial subtleties such as leading by example, mentoring, advising, counseling, suggesting, and recommending.

 How does "humanistic guiding" compare to humanistic management?

[According to Migneault] Both are actively concerned with human values, traits, and achievements. If *managing* is understood to mean directing, controlling, and handling people in their collective "entirety," then *guiding* should be understood to mean the orchestration of "parts"—expressed individual values or traits—for the benefit of the organization as a whole. Guiding is part of managing, but it focuses on using the expressed characteristics produced by people (the "individual") rather than focusing on managing people in a macro or mechanically expansive sense. Managing focuses on people advantage (people as a collective force). Guiding focuses on trait advantage (individual charac-teristics), a function of the former. All in all, whether the process is one of managing or one of guiding, the actions which the process represents translate into the ethical and effective orchestration of employees. Humanistic orchestration should be equated with hon-est and skillful managing of people, and with the guiding of human values and traits for legitimate institutional ends.

 What are the major operating principles of HMBT humanistic guiding?

[According to Migneault] There are eight fundamental principles:

1. The driving purpose of all HMBT effort at UNMGL is to ful-fill the organizational mission of UNMGL.

2. The organizational mission of UNMGL can be fulfilled only by its employees.

3. Managing, guiding, and orchestration are necessary to fulfill the organizational mission and to advance UNMGL in sup-port of the university's overall mission, goals, and objectives.

4. No employee in the organization should be underestimated.

5. UNMGL employees represent the gamut of individually pos-sessed human values, capacities, and traits.

6. Essentially, all individually expressed human values, capaci-ties, and traits are potentially useful.

7. Humanistic guiding orchestrates the individual employee's expressed values, capacities, and traits so that the collective workforce continuously yields more than the sum of its pro-ductive parts.

8. No HMBT practitioner must ever overestimate himself or herself.

 What have you accomplished with HMBT?

With HMBT, my colleagues and I have created and maintained an effective and efficient management system. With HMBT, the UNMGL faculty and staff have had the remarkable ability to ad-vance the university libraries in the face of ever-increasing demands and expectations and limited resources. With HMBT, library em-ployees have greatly improved library service and the ability of UNMGL to support higher levels of research. For example, in May 1995, the University of New Mexico Institute for Public Policy re-leased its findings regarding faculty and staff perceptions of the

University of New Mexico, including perceptions of the university libraries. With respect to "customer service," the university libraries received the highest ranking on campus. Prior to HMBT, ARL ranked the University of New Mexico libraries in 1987–1989 as being 102 out of 105. In less than seven years with HMBT, the libraries improved their ARL ranking significantly. As of this writing, the University of New Mexico libraries are ranked 53 out of 108.

 With HMBT, what have you accomplished regarding the humanistic welfare of library employees?

HMBT maintains unequivocal interest in employees as human beings, and in their individually expressed values, their capacities, and their stake in personal achievements. Accordingly, HMBT assumes that, as the individual functions, the individual places high personal value on his or her self-esteem and has inherent needs for being appreciated, for being respected, for having say when he or she wants to have say, for being listened to, for feeling wanted and useful—for being somebody. HMBT has responded well to these human values and needs to the continuous humanistic nourishment of the individual in the workplace. For example, HMBT has promoted broad-based empowerment of individuals so that they may assert themselves as individuals in the workplace. HMBT has invited and encouraged self-expression, setting self-imposed professional and academic standards, and taking the opportunity to celebrate in the workplace one's personal "humanness" without fear of reprisal, for example, from top library management.

 What have you done regarding implementing and fostering HMBT?

HMBT must be recognized for what it is; that is, HMBT represents a preference for a certain kind of managerial attitude, style, and behavior—humanistic. Considering everything that needs to be considered regarding the workplace in these times of ours, humanistic management can best be effected in a flat and flexible organizational arrangement that does not require extensive hierarchy and/or complex bureaucracy to function effectively. Humanistic management and management by teamwork fit as a perfect glove to a ready hand. At UNMGL, teams constitute the way in which the management system is structured, and humanistic management is the style or manner in which the teams are expected to function. UNMGL has several kinds of teams for a variety of purposes on different organizational levels, all of which share the responsibility for properly managing the organization as a whole. The model for all UNMGL teams to emulate is the Library Management Team (LMT) (i.e., the library's top management team). The Library Management Team was the first HMBT team established. As such, the Library Management Team was the primary mechanism for introducing, implementing, and fostering HMBT. The Library Management Team is an example still followed by other UNMGL teams.

The Library Management Team

 Describe the origins of the Library Management Team.

The Library Management Team is composed of the dean, associate dean, department heads, and others—in all, some 20 individuals. The team meets weekly, and the agenda is set and shared by all members. Although the dean presides more often than not, other members of the team may preside. Individuals lead the deliberations affecting their own specific agenda topics. Agendas are distributed to all library faculty, and notes of the deliberations are placed in the library's weekly newsletter. The Library Management Team serves several functions. It exists to work with the dean in running the library as a whole, as a forum for systemwide communication, as a place for shaking out new ideas, and as a place to learn of decisions for implementation.

 How are members of the Library Management Team selected?

The Library Management Team evolved from the Management Advisory Council (MANAC), composed of the dean, associate deans, and assistant deans who made up the Library Executive Committee, and library department heads. MANAC was advisory to the dean, and meetings were convened by the dean. This group and the Library Executive Committee were abolished when the Library Management Team was established. The Library Management Team has evolved into the library system's main policy-making group. Initially, individuals were members of the Library Management Team because they were members of the "old" Management Advisory Council or the "old" Library Executive Committee, or both. To a large extent, individuals are on the Library Management Team because they are department heads representing their given departments. In addition to fulfilling the roles as representatives of their given departments or area of influence, individuals were selected by the dean for their specialized knowledge, creativity, and problem-solving abilities.

Some individuals are on the team for purposes of staff development. Conceptually, anyone in the library system may be appointed to serve on the team.

 Describe the purpose of the Library Management Team (LMT).

The LMT provides managerial leadership regarding virtually all UNMGL operational matters, including determining library priorities, policies and procedures, and goals and objectives. The LMT serves as a communication forum for deliberating on virtually all library issues, including issues regarding organizational arrangement, equipment, personnel, budget allocation, performance evaluation, and library faculty and staff salary determination. The LMT is a lively, hands-on training academy for library managers. It serves as a model for team building, for improving one's ability to work with new or differing ideas, for problem solving, and for building professional camaraderie. Work permitting, LMT meetings (with limited exception) are open to all UNMGL employees.

 How large should the Library Management Team be?

The size of the Library Management Team is very much determined by its purposes. As long as individuals act professionally and earnestly wish to make it work, the size of the team can be relatively large. When the team was first formed (1986), it had 14 members. Eight years later, it had 20 members. Several individuals have said that the group is large enough, but a few have maintained that the team could be enlarged.

 How do you justify having that many librarians devoting so much time to team management meetings?

The Library Management Team meets weekly or semimonthly, depending on the time of year. At different managerial levels throughout the General Library, groups are encouraged to meet in teams to fulfill the goals and objectives of the library. It is true that librarians (and non-librarian staff) receiving relatively high salaries are frequently engaged in team meetings. Such meetings and associated personnel time are justified on the basis of measurable results, which take into consideration total quality management, cost-effectiveness, production, and service to constituencies. Compared with other ways of conducting business, team management meetings, specifically Humanistic Management by Teamwork, have thus far proven to be a most successful approach to organizing and running an academic research library.

Are there agendas for Library Management Team meetings?

Yes. Agendas are determined by input of LMT members and distributed widely. With some exceptions (sensitive personnel matters), LMT meetings are open to UNMGL employees (subject to work schedules). By looking at a given meeting's agenda, employees may decide whether to attend. Minutes, actually "notes," constitute the official record of LMT meetings. They, too, are distributed widely for public use—normally on a weekly basis. Openness to information is the rule; secrecy of information is the exception.

 How can a member of the library's management team be removed?

Removal of an individual from the Library Management Team could be, and has been, handled as a reassignment of duties.

 How does the Library Management Team avoid splitting into factions?

One could argue that some "factionalizing" does creep in from time to time, but it is quite minimal. Members of the Library Management Team have controlled whatever tendency there may have been for LMT to split into factions. Professionalism seems to rule. Controls prohibiting sustained factionalizing may be the result of peer pressure, as well as self-imposed discipline. Members of the Library Management Team are expected to participate actively during the group's deliberations, voicing their comments without prejudice. The give and take has been noteworthy. Preferably, decisions are reached on the basis of consensus. Voting on matters has been rare. On the few occasions when consensus could not be reached, the dean or the presiding officer of the given LMT meeting has had to break the deadlock and make a decision, a practice agreed to by the team.

 Is Humanistic Management by Teamwork practiced the same way in all of the departments, or is management by teamwork really a combination of team and hierarchical structures?

Not all managers and supervisors are naturally inclined to practice Humanistic Management by Teamwork or wish to be humanistic, at least not with every single dealing. More often than not, experienced library managers and supervisors have been trained in hierarchical environments. Humanistic Management by Teamwork does not come easily to some individuals. Hierarchical structures offer the "I am in charge" types more clearly defined accountability and authority.

Humanistic Management by Teamwork was largely superimposed as the umbrella managerial value on an array of internal, departmentalized hierarchical structures. Within each library department, Humanistic Management by Teamwork is practiced somewhat differently and is viewed as being in different levels of development. As each year passes, there is more management by teamwork, resulting in less hierarchy.

The Dean

 When is the dean required to exert authority?

There is the clear recognition that the library dean has the full authority to fulfill the responsibilities of the office of the dean. In the context of Humanistic Management by Teamwork and the Library Management Team, the dean's authority is shared. Authority is to be exerted cooperatively and without fuss. The dean has had to exert authority over or within the Library Management Team when decisions had to be made quickly or when consensus could not be reached, which has been rare. The dean is required to exercise authority on behalf of the university and when directed to do so by appropriate university authorities.

 How does the library dean begin to share authority?

Humanistic Management by Teamwork encourages the sharing of authority. Authority should be placed in the hands of those who are expected to fulfill specific responsibilities, matching accountability and responsibility. The Library Management Team is a good example. The team exists to provide leadership and sound management. All members of the team are expected to participate effectively as professional colleagues and peers. The idea is to appreciate consensus as being synonymous with authority, or "the" authority, vis-à-vis policy determination, problem solving, planning, action to be taken, decision making, and so on. The dean begins the sharing of authority by conscientiously letting go or, more accurately, releasing the relatively tight grip on the traditional, hierarchical reins of control. It is a matter of putting into practice, progressively, the themes of trust and risk taking. The dean's first step in sharing authority is to act beyond rhetoric.

When should the dean step in to resolve a problem?

Problems should be resolved as quickly as possible without causing new problems. Humanistic Management by Teamwork promotes a collective approach to problem solving, believing that the application of collective wisdom is generally the most thorough and effective approach. The dean does not always have to solve problems to be a dean, yet being a dean sometimes requires stepping in to resolve a problem. The dean must do so when the situation calls for it.

 What role does the dean have in planning?

The dean has a major role when it comes to planning, such as in the context of university-wide strategic planning, reallocation of university resources, planning for the future of the library. The dean is in a unique position to marshal an array of resources. The dean has an obligation to actively predict and anticipate future conditions, needs, and expectations on behalf of the library. The dean should skate where he/she believes the puck will be.

 Why should the dean be evaluated in the Humanistic Management by Teamwork environment?

The dean, perhaps more than anyone else in the library, must be accountable to library colleagues. Humanistic Management by Teamwork calls for an annual internal performance review of the dean by library colleagues and especially by the Library Management Team. The written upward evaluation of the dean's performance (as described in chapter 10) is forwarded to the provost. Humanistic Management by Teamwork has as one of its strengths the partnership approach and commitment to administering the library. Humanistic Management by Teamwork can only be its best when the dean is subject to evaluations by principals within the Library Management Team, library faculty, and staff at large. Should consensus reveal insufficient confidence in the dean, the dean should be willing to step aside.

 What budget information does the dean share and with whom?

The dean openly shares virtually all library budget information with all library employees. The dean actively shares budget information with members of the Library Management Team. Humanistic Management by Teamwork requires the dissemination of information, for without its widespread dissemination, availability, and access, sound management by teamwork is impossible. Free access to information, including the details of the budget, is at the heart of vertical, flat-lined administrative structures. At the University of New Mexico General Library, the budget is prepared and managed primarily by the Library Management Team.

 How widely is salary information distributed in the Humanistic Management by Teamwork environment?

All salary information pertaining to UNM employees is available to the public. The salaries of all UNM employees are noted in a public document, copies of which are available for perusal in the library. Salary determination for all library employees is done by the Library Management Team, including the awarding of merit pay and the correction of identified salary inequities.

 Describe the dean's external relationships.

The library dean is a member of the campuswide Deans Council. College deans and other university administrators (e.g., the president, vice presidents, top-level directors) view the library dean as administratively equivalent to the other academic deans on campus and assume that the library dean exercises his or her authority and power in a manner that is consistent with deans in general. HMBT is unique to the library, and it truly has little or no relevance to other units on campus. In effect, the library dean must work simultaneously in two administrative worlds, which are almost completely separate—each with its own protocols and expectations. Briefly, HMBT requires collegial, participatory, and shared administrative know-how. Dealing with entities and people "outside" the library requires the library dean to function more in accordance with traditional hierarchical policies and procedures.

Implementation at UNMGL

 How is hiring handled in the Humanistic Management by Teamwork environment?

The appointment of faculty is largely the responsibility of library faculty and the dean. The hiring of all library personnel is done in accordance with the policies and procedures set forth in the *University of New Mexico Faculty Handbook* and the *University of New Mexico Personnel Policy Handbook*. Faculty hirings are preceded by national searches and interviews conducted by the faculty. The dean has the authority for assigning responsibilities and duties and making reassignments when deemed necessary, usually in consultation with the Library Management Team. Faculty hirings for a specific department are usually heavily influenced by that department.

 What are the traits you look for in recruiting for the Humanistic Management by Teamwork environment?

People who perform well in situations characterized by ambiguity, uncertainty, and change do well in the team management environment. Recruiting should place priority on traits that reflect a genuine appreciation of diversity in people and the ability and willingness to complement the strengths of others. Persons are recruited who will succeed in an environment that values self-motivation, competent professionalism, appreciation for academic research librarianship, intellectual curiosity, ability to handle new and differing ideas, quality service to constituencies, cooperation, collaboration, and teamwork.

 What types of people are needed in the library administration of the Humanistic Management by Teamwork environment?

The Humanistic Management by Teamwork library can be best served administratively by people who are not biting at the bit to be the boss and are comfortable with the idea that the best authority to have is the kind that your colleagues and peers wish you to have. Recognizing the need for the ability to work effectively in a hierarchical bureaucracy, Humanistic Management by Teamwork library administrators must see value in linear administrative structures, the flatter the better. Egocentric and arrogant personalities, the "I get paid to make the decisions" type, need not apply. Authoritative or dictatorial leadership and Humanistic Management by Teamwork are antithetical. Humanistic Management by Teamwork administrators must be able to delegate, to share, and to give and take. They must be willing to serve as a resource for others, allow others to grow professionally, and allow others to be in the limelight. What is needed are people who are willing to listen, who are able to lead without flash, and who are sustained by quiet inner strength.

 How well do library faculty and library staff get along?

Very well. There are certain differences between library faculty and library staff. Faculty must meet the appointment, promotion, and retention criteria delineated in the *University of New Mexico Faculty*

Handbook. Library staff do not have the teaching, research, and service requirements, although in the Humanistic Management by Teamwork environment, staff are also professionals. "Professional" is defined by the manner in which one is expected to perform, not by the category of employment status. Both faculty and staff are encouraged to participate actively in governing the library, and both have access to funds for professional enrichment. Teams throughout the library are composed of both groups and, as a matter of fact, some staff are paid more than some faculty. Humanistic Management by Teamwork requires that faculty and staff work together as colleagues and team members.

 Do you think that Humanistic Management by Teamwork would work in a library where librarians are not faculty?

Even though management by teamwork has become a popular concept, Humanistic Management by Teamwork has yet to become a completely comfortable practice. One reason is because librarians are concerned about the image of librarianship as a profession. Both librarians and staff perform vocational library work, leading many library users to the conclusion that anyone working in a library is a librarian. For the purposes of professional status or recognition, librarians (MLS holders) have categorized themselves as professionals and have placed the non-MLS employee into a nonprofessional category, a stratification that makes teamwork difficult at best. This distinction does not seem to be as pronounced where librarians are faculty. Librarians who function as faculty and are characterized by teaching and research, including the requirement to publish, appear not as hard-pressed to make an issue over the professional-nonprofessional categorizations. All employees should and can be viewed as professionals, and Humanistic Management by Teamwork can then become increasingly viable.

 Why should librarians have faculty status?

Answering this question involves answering the following questions: How good a library does an institution of higher learning need or want? What kind of library can an institution afford? What kind of priority does an institution place on its library? If the answers come down to saying that the institution wants a library that is reasonably the best it can be, then the librarians onboard must be required to meet criteria at least comparable to criteria for the traditional teaching faculty on campus, and the librarians must be recognized as full faculty. Faculty criteria encourage, if not force, librarians to meet increasingly high professional and academic standards. Overall, such high standards make for better librarians, the result of which is a library that offers a higher quality of service in general. If an academic library is to succeed in fulfilling its mission in the face of limited resources, the library must be able to compete on the same field as the other academic units on campus. The library must be able to wield a certain amount of influence; it must be part of the academic community; and it must be effective regarding university or campus governance. An academic library can accomplish the things mentioned above only if its libraries are legitimately recognized as faculty.

 How can library faculty make a difference?

Library faculty must be more than faculty in name only. Ideally, library faculty must have impressive academic credentials and notable accomplishments in scholarship and research. They must be teachers as well as librarians. To recruit and retain such people, the working environment, conditions of employment, and (especially) salaries must be suitable. With this in mind, consider the following examples: At the University of New Mexico, library faculty have held or currently hold important positions on virtually all faculty committees. Librarians have chaired faculty senate committees (e.g., budget, graduate, undergraduate, curriculum, research policy, academic freedom, tenure). Librarians have been president and vice president of the University of New Mexico faculty senate. Librarians teach credit subject courses in a number of colleges. Librarians have been awarded campus research awards, including formal recognition as scholars. The library administers and operates the university-wide tutoring program, tutoring more than 5,000 students annually. Given the above, library faculty, their significant contributions, and the nature of their work have resulted in tremendous credibility for UNMGL. This, in turn, has helped the library obtain the support it needs—to advance its programs and services, and to fulfill its mission.

 How is Humanistic Management by Teamwork different from other management systems?

There are several distinct features of Humanistic Management by Teamwork that make UNMGL different from libraries characterized as hierarchical organizations. The Library Management Team structure; the performance appraisal system, which includes upward evaluations; the committee structure; the library faculty organization; and the empowerment of employees throughout the library—all create a climate that is conducive to growth and development. It is not possible to completely eliminate the pettiness, jealousies, and cruelty often found in the workplace, or to require all employees to leave their family or personal problems at home, but in an environment where individuals are treated as professionals with the respect and the dignity they deserve, the little problems do not often become big problems. The overall organizational climate at UNMGL is one full of trust, support, and respect. Humanistic Management by Teamwork does make the library a more humane workplace.

HMBT does not require or need a coterie of assistant deans or assistant directors. HMBT does not necessitate divisional compartmentalization, such as collection development, public services, and technical services. HMBT de-emphasizes the categorization of library personnel, such as "professional librarian" and "paraprofessional staff," and "library faculty" and "library support staff." Based on the manner in which all library employees are expected to behave and perform, HMBT assumes that all library employees are professional and are colleagues working as a team to fulfill the library's mission. HMBT fosters the practice of empowering all employees to be creative in their work. The HMBT environment is conducive to effecting outcomes assessment at all levels of the library organization, evidenced by the annual upward performance evaluation of all managers, including the dean. All library employees have an equal opportunity to participate in UNMGL governance. In the HMBT environment, UNMGL managers have the means to determine just what kind of library management system they want UNMGL to use. The preferred choice continues to be Humanistic Management by Teamwork.

Bibliography

Advances in Library Administration and Organization. Greenwich, Conn.: JAI Press, annual.

Bommer, M. R. W., and R. W. Chorba. *Decision Making for Library Management.* White Plains, N.Y.: Knowledge Industry Publications, 1982.

Brown, Nancy A. "Academic Libraries: An Operational Model for Participation." *Canadian Library Journal* 36 (August 1979): 201–7.

Burckel, Nicholas C. "Participatory Management in Academic Libraries: A Review." *College & Research Libraries* 45, no. 1 (January 1984): 25–34.

Butman, John. *FlyingFox: A Business Adventure in Teams and Teamwork.* New York: American Management Association, 1993.

Dickinson, D. W. "Some Reflections on Participative Management in Libraries." *College & Research Libraries* 39, no. 4 (July 1978): 253–62.

Drucker, Peter F. *Management: Tasks, Responsibilities, Practices*. New York: Harper & Row, 1974.

Dutton, B. G. "Staff Management and Staff Participation." In *A Reader in Library Management*, edited by Ross Shimmon, 129–45. London: Bingley, 1976.

Franklin, W. H. "Why You Can't Motivate Everyone." *Supervisory Management* 25 (April 1980): 21–28.

Grant, P. C. "Why Employee Motivation Has Declined in America." *Personnel Journal* 61 (December 1982): 905–9.

Hawkins, Katherine W. "Implementing Team Management in the Modern Library." *Library Administration & Management* 3, no. 1 (winter 1989): 11–15.

Kaplan, Louis. "The Literature of Participation: From Optimism to Realism." *College & Research Libraries* 36, no. 6 (November 1975): 473–79.

———. "On the Road to Participative Management: The American Academic Library, 1934–1970." *Libri* 38, no. 4 (1988): 314–20.

Lynch, Beverly P. "Participative Management in Relation to Library Effectiveness." *College & Research Libraries* 33, no. 5 (September 1972): 382–90.

MacCrimmon, Kenneth R., and Donald A. Ehrenburg, with W. T. Stanbury. *Taking Risks: The Management of Uncertainty*. New York: Free Press, 1986.

Marchant, Maurice P. "Participative Management, Job Satisfaction, and Service." *Library Journal* 107 (April 1982): 782–84.

———. *Participatory Management in Libraries*. Westport, Conn.: Greenwood, 1977.

Migneault, Robert LaLiberte. "Humanistic Management by Teamwork in Academic Libraries." *Library Administration & Management* 2, no. 3 (June 1988): 132–36.

Miles, Raymond E. *Theories of Management: Implications for Organizational Behavior and Development*. New York: McGraw-Hill, 1975.

Morgan, Gareth. *Images of Organizations*. Beverly Hills, Calif.: Sage Publications, 1986.

Reitz, H. Joseph. *Behavior in Organizations*. 3d ed. Homewood, Ill.: Dow Jones-Irwin, 1987.

Rooks, Dana C. *Motivating Today's Library Staff: A Management Guide.* Phoenix, Ariz.: Oryx Press, 1988.

Sager, Donald J. *Participatory Management in Libraries.* Metuchen, N.J.: Scarecrow Press, 1982.

Simon, Herbert A. *Administrative Behavior: A Study of the Decision-Making Processes in Administrative Organization.* 3d ed. New York: Free Press, 1976.

Smith, Kenwyn, and David N. Berg. *Paradoxes of Group Life: Understanding Conflict, Paralysis and Movement in Group Dynamics.* San Francisco: Jossey-Bass, 1987.

Stewart, Henry. "Staff Participation in the Management of Libraries and Its Relationship to Library Performance Characteristics." Ph.D. diss., Indiana University, 1972.

Webb, Gisela M. "Implementing Team Management at the Texas Tech University Libraries." *Library Personnel News* 1, no. 4 (fall 1987): 39–40.

●●●●●●●● Index

181